100 BEST FOODS TO STAY YOUNG

100 BEST FOODS TO STAY YOUNG

LOVE FOOD™

This edition published by Parragon Books Ltd in 2016 and distributed by

Parragon Inc.
440 Park Avenue South, 13th Floor
New York, NY 10016
www.parragon.com/lovefood

LOVE FOOD is an imprint of Parragon Books Ltd
Copyright © Parragon Books Ltd 2010–2016
LOVE FOOD and the accompanying heart device is a registered trademark of Parragon Books Ltd in
the USA, the UK, Australia, India, and the EU.

ISBN 978-1-4748-3786-6

Printed in China

Created and produced by Ivy Contract
New photography by Clive Streeter
Additional recipes by Judith Wills

Notes for the Reader
This book uses imperial, metric, and US cup measurements. Follow the same units of measurement
throughout; do not mix imperial and metric. All spoon measurements are level: teaspoons are assumed
to be 5 ml, and tablespoons are assumed to be 15 ml. Unless otherwise stated, milk is assumed to be
whole, eggs and individual vegetables such as potatoes are medium, and pepper is freshly ground
black pepper.

The nutritional information is based on measurements of 100 g/3½ oz or by the number of items stated;
however, some of these measurements have been converted to cups for the reader. These are not
exact conversions but will give the reader an idea of the size of the serving.

The times given are an approximate guide only. Preparation times differ according to the techniques
used by different people and the cooking times may also vary from those given as a result of the type
of oven used. Optional ingredients, variations, or serving suggestions have not been included in the
calculations.

Medical and pharmaceutical knowledge is constantly changing and the author(s) and the publisher
cannot and do not guarantee the accuracy or appropriateness of the contents of this book;
In any event, this book is not intended to be, and should not be relied upon, as a substitute for advice
from your healthcare practitioner before making any major dietary changes;
Food Allergy Disclaimer: The author(s) and the publisher are not responsible for any adverse reactions
to the recipes contained herein.
The statements in this book have not been evaluated by the U.S. Food and Drug Administration. This
book is not intended to treat, cure or prevent any disease.
For the reasons set out above, and to the fullest extent permitted by law, the author(s) and the
publisher: (i) cannot and do not accept any legal duty of care or responsibility in relation to the
accuracy of appropriateness of the contents of this book, even where expressed as "advice" or using
other words to this effect; and (ii) disclaim any liability, loss, damage or risk that may be claimed or
incurred as a consequence—directly or indirectly—of the use and/or application of any of the contents
of this book.

CONTENTS

INTRODUCTION

Good nutrition is the foundation of a youthful, vital body that is able to work to its full capacity. The right foods are the key to staying young, inside and out. The results show in how you look, in how you feel, and in your quality of life.

How can our bodies and minds stay young?

Staying young means helping your body constantly repair and renew, not only to recover from the stresses of the day, but also to supply the building blocks and nutrients that we need all the time to build new cells. Every part of your body is being continually replaced, and factors, such as stress, exercise, sunlight, junk food, computers, TVs, and pollution work to stop that from happening by depleting nutrients or damaging cells and tissues.

By eating to stay young, you can take the energy, weight, movement, strength, mental agility, and outlook that you had when younger into your senior years. It is natural to age, but we can avoid this happening prematurely by consuming the healthiest food possible. The foods with the most nutrients and the least damaging potential are unprocessed foods that come straight from nature. These are the foods we have evolved to live with, and which work with our bodies for optimal health.

Holistic focus

This book identifies the different aspects of health that are needed to safeguard vitality and youthfulness. All of the recipes satisfy these categories to an extent, but each has been coded to indicate its particular potency.

(S) **Skin, hair, and nails**—the health of the inside of your body is reflected on the outside. Poor health shows up as dull, blemished skin, wrinkles, and age spots. Maintaining your appearance is also a good incentive to stay motivated to eat well.

(M) **Mobility and strength**—good posture, reactions, and pain-free movement keep you from feeling old and from being less able to enjoy the activities that keep you young at heart.

(D) **Digestive/detoxification health**—these systems operate in tandem to use the nutritional elements you need to stay young, and eliminate harmful toxins and bacteria that can make you feel sluggish and bloated. The presence of beneficial, probiotic bacteria in the digestive system is key to staying young.

(B) **Brain health**—your brain needs fuel and nutrients for you to stay happy and be able to concentrate and remember efficiently. Good mental health motivates you to look after yourself. Much of how young you feel comes down to perception.

(H) **Heart health**—your heart keeps your blood pumping and circulating, taking oxygen and nutrients to every cell in the body in order to renew and rejuvenate.

(I) **Immunity-supporting antioxidant**—antioxidants mop up harmful, unstable molecules that derive from factors, such as pollution and stress. These play a major part in enabling your immune system to protect you from invading elements and from becoming oversensitive, which leads to allergies. These substances also help reduce inflammation, the root cause of most diseases and premature aging.

The importance of a varied diet and healthy lifestyle
The age-defying foods featured in this book work together, so make sure you benefit from a whole spectrum of nutrients by choosing a varied and colorful diet. Nutrition is crucial to staying young, but other factors are also important. Exercise, relaxation, laughter, socializing, sunlight, and breathing well in clean air all combine to help you feel happy and youthful for longer.

FRUITS

Fruits provide a wealth of rejuvenating nutrients and fiber. We have evolved to be drawn to their sweetness because our bodies need their abundant vitamin C. Two or three palm-size portions of fruit a day are all that's necessary to reap the benefits of nature's healthy sweet treats.

(S) Skin, hair, and nails

(M) Mobility and strength

(D) Digestive/detoxification health

(B) Brain health

(H) Heart health

(I) Immunity-supporting antioxidant

01

AVOCADOS

The avocado is a true superfood. Its creamy flesh is packed with nutrients that keep the skin looking youthful and the heart strong.

DID YOU KNOW?

The name avocado comes from the Aztec word for testicle, *ahuacatl*. Its shape and its vitamin E content have given it a reputation as a fertility fruit (the Latin name for vitamin E, *tocopherol*, means fertility).

MAJOR NUTRIENTS PER MEDIUM-SIZE AVOCADO

Calories	320
Total fat	29.47 g
Monounsaturated fat	19.7 g
Protein	4.02 g
Carbohydrate	17.15 g
Fiber	13.5 g
Vitamin A	393 IU
Vitamin B_6	2.7 mg
Vitamin C	12 g
Vitamin E	4.16 mg
Copper	0.52 mg
Magnesium	58 mg
Folate	163 mcg
Lutein/Zeaxanthin	545 mcg

Avocados often get a negative press because of their high fat content, but fat comes in many different forms and some is necessary for good health. This rich fruit contains healthy monounsaturated fats and fat-soluble nutrients, including vitamins A and E, that are essential for the health of our fatty body parts, such as the skin, eyes, heart, brain, and liver. For a fruit, avocados also have good protein content. This combines with the vitamin C, B vitamins, and copper in avocado to support the production of collagen, the substance from which all body tissues are made. Collagen is vital for skin, bone, and muscle rejuvenation, and helps reduce wrinkles.

- Contain beneficial fats, vitamins, minerals, and plant chemicals, which work in combination to support heart health.
- High levels of the carotenoid nutrient, lutein, protect the eyes from age-related macular degeneration and the skin from the wrinkles and pigment changes caused by sun damage.
- Included in the Mediterranean diet, which is famed for its life-sustaining properties. The healthy monounsaturated fat of avocado is also found in olives, nuts, and seeds.

Practical tips:
The texture of avocados makes them the perfect alternative to more sugary bananas in smoothies. If mixed with other fruits, the fat content of the avocado will slow down the release of the sugars from the fruits, making an even more substantial drink.

Smoked salmon, avocado, and arugula salad

SERVES 6

7 oz/200 g fresh asparagus spears
1 large ripe avocado
1 tbsp lemon juice
large handful of fresh arugula
    leaves
8 oz/225 g smoked salmon slices
1 red onion, finely sliced
1 tbsp chopped fresh parsley
1 tbsp chopped fresh chives

Dressing

1 garlic clove, chopped
4 tbsp extra virgin olive oil
2 tbsp white wine vinegar
1 tbsp lemon juice
1 tsp mustard

Method

1 Bring a large saucepan of lightly salted water to a boil. Add the asparagus and cook for 4 minutes, then drain. Refresh under cold running water and drain again. Set aside to cool.

2 To make the dressing, combine all the ingredients in a small bowl and stir together well. Cut the avocado in half lengthwise, then remove and discard the pit and skin. Cut the flesh into bite-size pieces and brush with lemon juice to prevent discoloration of the fruit.

3 To assemble the salad, arrange the arugula leaves on individual serving plates and top with the asparagus and avocado. Cut the smoked salmon into strips and scatter over the top of the salad, then scatter over the onion and herbs. Drizzle over the dressing and serve.

02

BANANAS

The banana is the ultimate sports snack because it provides quick, quality fuel. It is perfect for replenishing flagging cells and ensuring youthful repair to the body.

Bananas are undeniably high in sugar, but they shouldn't be underestimated for their health-giving antiaging properties. A ripe banana contains a high amount of fiber, including the prebiotic inulin, which feeds our beneficial (probiotic) digestive tract bacteria, the first line of defense for the immune system. Keeping your digestive tract bacteria healthy can help prevent inflammatory conditions, such as eczema, asthma, and arthritis, and support the digestion and absorption of nutrients needed to retain optimal health and keep you looking and feeling young.

- Potassium and vitamin C help transport oxygen around the body to renew and revitalize the skin.
- Contain high levels of potassium, vitamin C, and vitamin B_6, which are all important for heart health. Athletes draw on this rich mix to support performance, recovery, and muscle response.
- Shown to help kidney function and eliminate fluid retention, reducing puffiness for a more youthful appearance.

Practical tips:
The fruit of choice for many people with a sweet tooth, bananas are best eaten when the skin is a solid yellow color, with no bruises. Avoid overripe bananas as, by this stage, the sugars will have broken down and the fruit becomes too sweet. Bananas may not be suitable for people with phlegm and nasal congestion as they can make these conditions worse.

DID YOU KNOW?

The name banana comes from the Arabic *banan* or "finger;" they grow in clusters of up to 20 fruit called a "hand."

MAJOR NUTRIENTS PER MEDIUM-SIZE BANANA

Calories	105
Total fat	0.39 g
Protein	1.29 g
Carbohydrate	26.95 g
Fiber	3.1 g
Vitamin B_6	0.43 mg
Vitamin C	10.3 mg
Potassium	422 mg

Banana and strawberry smoothie

SERVES 2

1 just ripe banana, sliced
heaping ¾ cup hulled strawberries
⅔ cup plain live yogurt

Method

1 Put the banana, strawberries, and yogurt into a food processor or blender and process for a few seconds until smooth. Pour into glasses and serve at once.

03 RASPBERRIES

Bursting with vitamin C and proanthocyanidins, raspberries have one of the highest antioxidant, antiaging profiles of any fruit.

Raspberries are packed with the red/purple antioxidant proanthocyanidins, which are the most abundant antioxidant in the plant kingdom. They support circulation and, in combination with vitamin C, aid memory and heart function, as well as contributing to the health and vitality of your veins, skin, and hair. Studies suggest that raspberries have positive effects on mood and concentration. These wonder berries have high levels of the antioxidant ellagic acid, which supports liver detoxification, along with good amounts of fiber, which also helps to rid the body of aging toxins.

- Ellagic acid moves bile through the liver, helping to regulate cholesterol and keep the heart young.
- Low starch and high fiber content provides sustained levels of energy and keeps cravings at bay to maintain a youthful weight.
- High antioxidant capacity derives from substances, such as quercetin, catechins, gallic acid, and salycilic acid, which prevent premature aging.

Practical tips:
Raspberries can be taken straight from the freezer and processed in the blender to make delicious smoothies. Like most berries, they have been less adulterated by modern breeding methods than other fruits, so they have a naturally lower sugar content (as their tart taste suggests). Buy in season from local growers to benefit most from their nutrient content, and choose the darkest berries.

DID YOU KNOW?

A large percentage of a raspberry's weight is fiber, which helps to remove toxins from the body. Fiber is as important as antioxidant content in the pursuit of staying young.

MAJOR NUTRIENTS PER ¾ CUP RASPBERRIES

Calories	52
Total fat	0.65 g
Protein	1.2 g
Carbohydrate	11.94 g
Fiber	6.5 g
Vitamin C	26.2 mg
Potassium	151 mg
Lutein/Zeaxanthin	136 mcg

Raspberry and feta salad with couscous

SERVES 6

*2 cups couscous or barley
   couscous*
*2½ cups boiling chicken or low-salt
   vegetable stock*
scant 3 cups raspberries
small bunch of fresh basil
*1½ cups crumbled or cubed,
   drained feta cheese*
2 zucchini, thinly sliced
*4 scallions, trimmed
   and diagonally sliced*
*scant ½ cup pine nuts, lightly
   toasted*
grated rind of 1 lemon

Dressing

1 tbsp white wine vinegar
1 tbsp balsamic vinegar
4 tbsp extra virgin olive oil
juice of 1 lemon
salt and pepper

Method

1 Put the couscous in a large, heatproof bowl and pour over the stock. Stir well, cover, and let soak until all the stock has been absorbed.
2 Pick over the raspberries, discarding any that are overripe.
3 Shred the basil leaves.
4 Transfer the couscous to a large serving bowl and stir well to break up any lumps. Add the cheese, zucchini, scallions, raspberries, and pine nuts.
5 Stir in the basil and lemon rind and toss all the ingredients together in the bowl.
6 Put all the dressing ingredients in a screw-top jar, with salt and pepper to taste, screw on the lid, and shake until well blended. Pour over the salad and serve.

04

PEACHES

The soft fruit of this member of the rose family makes a nutritional sweet substitute for aging refined sugars and provides skin-nourishing nutrients.

Like most orange fruit and vegetables, peaches are abundant in carotenoid nutrients, the antioxidants that protect fatty areas of the body, in our liver, skin, heart, and other organs, including the brain, which is 60 percent fat. These fatty areas are susceptible to damage and we rely on fat-soluble antioxidants, such as carotenoids and vitamin A, to slow down degeneration and aging. Peaches are also high in vitamin C, which protects what are known as watery areas of the body, in and between cells and in the bloodstream. The high boron content of peaches has been shown to promote new bone growth and reduce the risk of prostate cancer in men.

- Rich in potassium, vitamin C, and iron, important for circulation and taking oxygen around the body to renew and revitalize skin.
- Their gentle laxative effect helps maintain bowel regularity, ensuring the removal of aging toxins.
- Contain the minerals magnesium and phosphorus, used by the nervous system for optimum brain and muscle function.

Practical tips:
Choose fruit that is still firm and only just becoming soft, with yellowy-cream coloring between the red areas and a velvety skin. Look for bruises as they spread quickly, and wash only immediately before eating as any damage to the skin can accelerate spoiling.

DID YOU KNOW?

Peaches have long been considered a medicinal plant and are recommended during convalescence for those with fatigue or depression.

MAJOR NUTRIENTS PER MEDIUM-SIZE PEACH

Calories	58
Total fat	0.38 g
Protein	1.36 g
Carbohydrate	14.31 g
Fiber	2.2 g
Vitamin C	9.9 mg
Vitamin A	489 IU
Potassium	285 mg
Phosphorus	30 mg
Beta-carotene	243 mcg
Iron	0.38 mg
Magnesium	13.7 mg
Lutein/Zeaxanthin	136 mcg

Fruity stuffed peaches

SERVES 4

4 ripe but firm peaches
1 cup blueberries
scant 1 cup raspberries
⅔ cup freshly squeezed
   orange juice
1–2 tsp good-quality honey,
   or to taste
1 tbsp brandy (optional)
generous ¾ cup live Greek-style
   yogurt
1 tbsp finely grated orange rind

Method

1 Preheat the oven to 350°F/180°C. Cut the peaches in half, remove the pits, then place in a shallow ovenproof dish.

2 Mix the blueberries and raspberries together in a bowl and use to fill the hollows left by the removal of the peach pits. Spoon any extra berries around.

3 Mix together the orange juice and honey, and brandy, if using, in a small bowl and pour the mixture over the fruit. Blend the yogurt with the grated orange rind in another bowl and let chill in the refrigerator until required.

4 Bake the berry-filled peaches for 10 minutes, or until the fruit is hot. Serve with the orange-flavored yogurt.

05 STRAWBERRIES

Strawberries contain more fiber than the equivalent weight of whole wheat bread, making them very effective at removing aging toxins from the body.

Along with carrots, peas, and the cabbage family, strawberries contain lignans, which bind with bile acids in the liver to help regulate cholesterol and stop the build up of gallstones, and may also help prevent colon cancer. Strawberries are phytoestrogens: foods that balance female hormones by binding excess estrogens to a protein in the blood. This action reduces the amount of estrogen in sensitive tissue and places it where it is needed. It also helps protect the skin from becoming dry and losing elasticity with age.

- High ellagic acid content provides antioxidant action and the removal of toxins from the body, giving a double boost to skin health.
- The seeds on the outside of the fruit contain cleansing fiber and healing nutrients, including zinc and the B vitamins.
- Excellent source of vitamin C and potassium, supporting vital heart health and youthful bone density.

Practical tip:
To preserve their vitamin C content, buy strawberries with the stems attached and don't remove these until eating. Look for any mold on the berries as it can spread very rapidly. Frozen strawberries can be used to sweeten yogurt in place of sugar, as they release some juice when defrosted.

DID YOU KNOW?

Strawberries are the first fruit to ripen in spring. They are the most popular berry, making them easy to add to a healthy diet, especially as a sweet treat.

MAJOR NUTRIENTS PER ⅔ CUP SLICED STRAWBERRIES

Calories	32
Total fat	0.3 g
Protein	0.67 g
Carbohydrate	7.68 g
Fiber	2 g
Vitamin C	58.8 mg
Vitamin B_3	0.39 mg
Vitamin B_6	0.47 mg
Vitamin K	15 mcg
Potassium	153 mg
Folate	24 mcg
Zinc	0.14 mg
Lutein/Zeaxanthin	26 mcg

Melon and strawberry salad

SERVES 4

½ iceberg lettuce, shredded
1 small honeydew melon
heaping 1⅓ cups sliced
    strawberries
2-inch/5-cm piece cucumber,
    thinly sliced
fresh mint sprigs, for garnishing

Dressing

generous ¾ cup plain live yogurt
2-inch/5-cm piece cucumber, peeled
a few fresh mint leaves
½ tsp finely grated lime or
    lemon rind
3–4 ice cubes

Method

1 Arrange the shredded lettuce
  on 4 serving plates.
2 Cut the melon lengthwise
  into quarters. Scoop out the
  seeds and cut through the
  flesh down to the skin at
  1-inch/2.5-cm intervals.
  Cut the melon close to the
  skin and detach the flesh.
3 Place the chunks of melon
  on the shredded lettuce
  with the strawberries and
  cucumber slices.

4 To make the dressing, put
  the yogurt, cucumber, mint
  leaves, lime or lemon rind, and
  ice cubes into a blender or
  food processor. Blend together
  for about 15 seconds, until
  smooth. Alternatively, chop
  the cucumber and mint
  finely, crush the ice cubes,
  and combine with the
  other ingredients.
5 Serve the salad with a
  little dressing poured over it.
  Garnish with sprigs of
  fresh mint.

06 PASSION FRUIT

A great all-rounder, passion fruit is full of powerful antioxidants, such as the healing vitamins A and C, which take action in the body to slow down the signs of aging.

High in the orange spectrum of antioxidants, the vitamin A and beta-carotene content of passion fruit gives skin a youthful boost. Enjoying this fruit will also protect your skin against the sun and help avoid sun damage, such as pigment changes and lines. Although we need some sunlight for health, especially to enhance mood, and to encourage restorative sleep cycles and bone health, we are damaged by its UV rays when it hits the skin. Many fruits, especially tropical fruits, such as passion fruit, that receive intense amounts of sunlight, contain vitamin A and carotenoid antioxidants to protect themselves against UV rays as they ripen. By eating these fruits, we reap the same sun-protecting properties, while also satisfying our requirements for high amounts of vitamin C.

- High levels of potassium, fiber, and vitamin C combine to prevent heart disease.
- A highly alkalizing fruit, which helps fluid balance and detoxification, crucial for maintaining a youthful appearance.
- Vitamin C helps knit together the collagen that keeps skin plump and wrinkle-free.

Practical tip:
The seeds of passion fruit are edible, so you can scoop out the entire contents from the skin and enjoy as a delicious snack. When made into juice or to flavor foods, the seeds are usually removed. Keep the ripe fruit in the refrigerator for up to a week.

DID YOU KNOW?

The yellow variety of this nutrient-rich fruit has more antioxidant carotenoids and is made into juice, while the purple variety has more vitamin C and is sold as fresh produce.

MAJOR NUTRIENTS PER MEDIUM-SIZE PASSION FRUIT

Calories	17
Total fat	0.13 g
Protein	0.40 g
Carbohydrate	4.21 g
Fiber	1.9 g
Vitamin A	229 IU
Vitamin C	5.4 mg
Beta-carotene	134 mcg
Potassium	63 mg

Passion fruit smoothie

SERVES 2

2 peaches
1 cup red grapes
heaping ¾ cup strawberries
1 passion fruit
seeds from ½ vanilla bean

Method

1 Halve and pit the peaches and process or blend with the grapes and strawberries.
2 Halve the passion fruit and scoop out the flesh, scrape the seeds from the vanilla bean, and stir both into the juice.
3 Pour into glasses and serve.

07

PAPAYA

Papaya contains papain, a protein-digesting enzyme that counteracts digestive disorders and inflammation, helping reduce these aging factors.

Papain has been used in the countries where papaya grows for centuries to treat a multitude of digestive disorders. More recently, it has featured as an ingredient in digestive enzyme supplements, which are taken to help break down food. Papaya is an antiaging, rejuvenating food because of its ability to help the body receive the maximum level of nutrients by aiding digestion and absorption, both crucial for staying young.

- Contains the carotenoid lycopene, which may help prevent the spread of cancer cells.
- Papaya seeds have an antibacterial effect, keeping damaging, aging bacteria at bay.
- High in calcium and potassium, which together help regulate blood pressure and fluid balance, reducing bloating and puffiness for a youthful appearance.
- Contains the amino acid arginine, which supports heart function, helping it stay strong throughout life.

Practical tips:
Papaya powders or purees, and supplements in capsule form, can be bought for use as digestive aids. Eating raw papaya after a course of antibiotics is thought to help restore the natural, beneficial bacteria of the digestive system. Papaya is often combined with pineapple so that its properties can be further enhanced by pineapple's protein-digesting enzyme bromelain.

DID YOU KNOW?

Papaya is often called "pawpaw" in Asia, but this is not to be confused with the North American pawpaw, which is a different, much larger fruit.

MAJOR NUTRIENTS PER MEDIUM-SIZE PAPAYA

Calories	120
Total fat	0.4 g
Protein	1.5 g
Carbohydrate	30 g
Fiber	5.5 g
Calcium	73 mg
Potassium	780 mg
Beta-carotene	839 mcg
Lutein/Zeaxanthin	228 mcg

Papaya salad

SERVES 6 (D) (I)

1 crisp lettuce
¼ small white cabbage
2 papayas
2 tomatoes
¼ cup roughly chopped peanuts
4 scallions, trimmed and
  thinly sliced
basil leaves, for garnishing

Dressing

4 tbsp extra virgin olive oil
1 tbsp Thai fish sauce or light
  soy sauce
2 tbsp lime or lemon juice
1 tsp dark brown sugar
1 tsp finely chopped fresh red
  or green chile

Method

1 To make the dressing, whisk together the oil, fish sauce, lime juice, sugar, and chile. Set aside, stirring occasionally to dissolve the sugar.
2 Shred the lettuce and white cabbage, then toss together and arrange on a large serving plate.
3 Peel the papayas and slice them in half. Scoop out the seeds, then slice the flesh thinly. Arrange on top of the lettuce and cabbage.
4 Soak the tomatoes in a bowl of boiling water for 1 minute, then lift out and peel. Remove the seeds and chop the flesh. Arrange the tomatoes on top of the lettuce and cabbage.
5 Scatter the peanuts and scallions over the top. Whisk the dressing and pour over the salad. Garnish with basil leaves and serve at once.

08

OLIVES

Olives offer the same health benefits as olive oil, but with extra phytosterols, lutein, and vitamins A and E for an added antiaging boost.

MAJOR NUTRIENTS PER 1 CUP PITTED OLIVES

Calories	145
Total fat	15.32 g
Monounsaturated fat	11.3 g
Omega-6 fatty acids	1,215 mg
Omega-9 fatty acids	11,145 mg
Protein	1.03 g
Carbohydrate	3.84 g
Fiber	3.3 g
Vitamin A	393 IU
Vitamin E	3.81 mg
Beta-carotene	231 mcg
Lutein/Zeaxanthin	510 mcg
Sodium	1,556 mg
Phytosterols	176 mg

The fatty nature of olives makes them a fantastic carrier of the fat-soluble nutrients that are so important for forming and protecting every single cell membrane in the body. This translates as wrinkle prevention, bone strength, and brain clarity. The valuable oil within the olives moves these nutrients through the digestive system so that they can be absorbed and used where needed. Taken together, the monounsaturated fats, omega-6 fatty acids, vitamins, and carotenoids in olives provide staunch support for all-round heart health. The only downside of this food is the high sodium content, which needs balancing out with potassium from other foods for the body to retain good blood pressure.

- Contain lutein and vitamin A to protect the eyes from macular degeneration, a condition associated with older age.
- Vitamins A and E ensure skin is kept lubricated; dry skin can wrinkle and age more easily.
- Vitamin E may help prevent cancer and keeps blood vessels healthily dilated.

Practical tips:
Olives come in a wide range of varieties, not only green and black. Try sampling some of the different sizes, flavorings, and preparations at a good-quality farmer's market or deli to discover your personal preference, and to find out which go best with other foodstuffs and drinks. Olives with pits retain their flavor better.

Olives with orange and lemon

SERVES 6

2 tsp fennel seeds
2 tsp cumin seeds
heaping 1¼ cups green olives
heaping 1¼ cups black olives
2 tsp grated orange rind
2 tsp grated lemon rind
3 shallots, finely chopped
pinch of ground cinnamon

Dressing

4 tbsp white wine vinegar
5 tbsp extra virgin olive oil
2 tbsp freshly squeezed
    orange juice
1 tbsp chopped fresh mint
1 tbsp chopped fresh parsley

Method

1 Dry-fry the fennel seeds and cumin seeds in a small, heavy-bottom skillet, shaking the pan frequently, until they begin to pop and give off their aroma. Remove the skillet from the heat and let cool.

2 Place the olives, orange and lemon rinds, shallots, cinnamon, and toasted seeds in a bowl.

3 To make the dressing, whisk the vinegar, olive oil, orange juice, mint, and parsley together in a bowl and pour over the olives. Toss well, cover, and let chill for 1–2 days before serving.

09 PRUNES

A prune is any species of dried plum. They are highly concentrated sources of fiber and are very effective at flushing aging toxins out of the body.

The host of antioxidants contained in prunes ensures that they are very high on the ORAC (Oxygen Radical Absorbance Capacity) index. Most of these protective and disease-preventing antioxidants are phenolic compounds, or water-soluble antioxidants, such as vitamin C and rutin, both of which keep your veins healthy and help prevent bruising and varicose veins, support circulation and heart function, and transport nutrients to the skin for healing. Prunes and prune juice are common home remedies for constipation, partly because of their fiber content: the soluble fiber helps speed up toxic waste elimination, and the insoluble fiber helps to bulk out stools.

- The insoluble fiber in prunes make you feel full, and thus they regulate appetite to help you maintain youthful weight levels.
- Prunes release their sugars very slowly, preventing these sugars from causing accelerated aging of the skin.
- About 60 percent of the soluble fiber in prunes comes from pectin, which helps remove damaging and aging toxic metals, such as lead and mercury, from the body.

Practical tips:
Make a simple puree by blending prunes and dried apricots with some boiling water and cinnamon in a blender. This less sugary alternative to jam makes a great sweetener for yogurt and oatmeal. Prunes work well in savory dishes, such as Moroccan tagines, providing complementary sweet tones to slow-cooked meats.

DID YOU KNOW?

In recent times, the popularity of prunes as a culinary ingredient has increased. This may be partly due to a campaign by the commercial growers, which has remarketed them as "dried plums."

MAJOR NUTRIENTS PER ¾ CUP PITTED PRUNES

Calories	240
Total fat	0.38 g
Protein	2.18 g
Carbohydrate	63.88 g
Fiber	7.1 g
Calcium	43 mg
Magnesium	41 mg
Beta-carotene	394 mcg
Lutein/Zeaxanthin	148 mcg

Prune oat muffins

MAKES 12 (B) (I)

light olive oil or melted butter,
    for greasing (if using)
1 cup whole wheat flour
1 tbsp baking powder
heaping ½ cup light brown sugar
heaping ½ cup rolled oats
heaping ¾ cup chopped pitted
    prunes
2 eggs
heaping 1 cup buttermilk
6 tbsp light olive oil
1 tsp vanilla extract

Method

1 Preheat the oven to 400°F/200°C. Grease a 12-cup muffin pan or line with 12 paper liners. Sift together the flour and baking powder into a large bowl. Stir in the sugar, oats, and chopped prunes.

2 Lightly beat the eggs in a large pitcher or bowl, then beat in the buttermilk, oil, and vanilla extract. Make a well in the center of the dry ingredients and pour in the beaten liquid ingredients. Stir gently until just combined; do not overmix.

3 Spoon the batter into the prepared muffin pan. Bake in the preheated oven for about 20 minutes, until well risen, golden brown, and firm to the touch.

4 Let the muffins cool in the pan for 5 minutes, then serve warm or transfer to a wire rack and let cool.

10

WATERMELON

Watermelon has beneficial effects on the body's fluid balance, helping prevent water retention and promoting well-hydrated youthful skin.

Watermelon has long been used in tropical countries to quench thirst, with the supporting effect of helping the body to shed excess fluid, which is often held in the face, hands, ankles, and feet and causes bloating and puffiness. As the watermelon is 92 percent water, its 6 percent of sugar stays well diluted, and does not negatively affect blood-sugar levels, but instead helps to pull water into the cells. This action keeps skin and organs well hydrated, which is crucial to retaining youthfulness. The bright red color of the flesh is due to the watermelon's high levels of the carotenoid antioxidants beta-carotene and lycopene, which help protect skin from the damage caused by the sun's UV rays.

- Diuretic effect helps clean out the kidneys, thus supporting revitalizing detoxification.
- The amino acid arginine takes sugars out of the bloodstream for use as energy, helping to regulate weight.
- Excellent source of vitamin C for healing all body tissues and keeping skin plump and free of age spots.

Practical tips:
Choose watermelons with skin that looks smooth and dull. They should sound hollow when tapped, then reveal strong red-colored flesh inside with no white streaks, and dark brown or black seeds. Eat slices of watermelon to cool down on a hot day, or make juice by scooping out the seeds and blending the flesh.

DID YOU KNOW?

Cubic watermelons, grown in glass boxes, have been developed in Japan because they are easier to stack and store than the natural, spherical fruit.

MAJOR NUTRIENTS PER ⅔ CUP DICED WATERMELON

Calories	30
Total fat	0.15 g
Protein	0.61 g
Carbohydrate	7.55 g
Fiber	0.4 g
Vitamin C	8.1 mg
Potassium	112 mg
Lycopene	4,532 mcg
Beta-carotene	303 mcg

Watermelon and pomegranate salad

SERVES 4–6

1 small ripe watermelon or 1 large
    wedge, about 3 lb 5 oz/1.5 kg
1 ripe pomegranate
1 tbsp rosewater
1–2 tsp good-quality honey
    (optional)
fresh mint leaves, for garnishing

Method

1 Remove the skin and seeds from the watermelon. Put the flesh on
  a plate to catch the juice and cut it into bite-size cubes. Put the
  cubes into a bowl or serving dish.

2 Cut the pomegranate open on the same plate to catch the juice
  and scoop out the seeds, discarding any of the bitter membrane
  and pith. Add the seeds to the watermelon.

3 Pour the watermelon and pomegranate juices into a bowl and stir
  in the rosewater. If using, stir in the honey until it has dissolved.

4 Pour the scented juice over the fruit and toss lightly. Cover and chill
  in the refrigerator for at least 1 hour. Scatter the mint leaves over
  the top to garnish and serve chilled.

11

KIWI

The kiwi has an unusual amount of healthy omega-3 fatty acids for a fruit. This, combined with its high vitamin C content, helps maintain youthful heart function.

Eating the edible seeds of fruits is extremely beneficial, and the seeds of the kiwi are particularly easy to swallow. As well as fiber and zinc, seeds contain all the nutrients and enzymes needed for a plant to grow, and taking them into our bodies means we are able to grow and rejuvenate, too. Kiwi seeds contain on average 62 percent alpha-linoleic acid, the omega-3 fatty acid that helps protect the heart and decrease inflammation, inside and outside the body, so preventing the diseases associated with aging. Kiwi is also a good source of copper, which is needed for collagen production and, therefore, healthy skin, nails, and muscles.

- Comparable to a banana in terms of high potassium content, keeping kidneys healthy so they can remove aging toxins.
- Contains more vitamin C than oranges, as well as vitamin E and rehydrating omega-3 fatty acids for a skin-nourishing combination.
- Vitamin C works with copper to produce collagen, to keep skin renewed and firm.

Practical tips:

Kiwis can be eaten whole like an apple: eating the skin means you don't miss out on the vitamin C that lies just beneath the skin, and vastly increases the fruit's insoluble fiber and antioxidant content. To test if a kiwi is ripe, press it. You should be able to depress the skin slightly. Dried kiwi slices make healthy snacks, and can be bought in health food stores and supermarkets.

DID YOU KNOW?

Studies have shown that kiwi may relieve symptoms of respiratory conditions, such as asthma and coughs. Healthy breathing is crucial for rejuvenation and staying young throughout life.

MAJOR NUTRIENTS PER MEDIUM-SIZE KIWI

Calories	46
Total fat	0.39 g
Protein	0.85 g
Carbohydrate	11.06 g
Fiber	2.26 g
Vitamin C	69.9 mg
Vitamin E	1.10 mg
Potassium	235 mg
Copper	0.10 mcg
Calcium	22.66 mg
Zinc	25.64 mg
Omega-3	31.75 mg

Kiwi smoothie

SERVES 2

1 mango
4 kiwi
1½ cups pineapple juice
4 fresh mint leaves

Method

1 Cut the mango into 2 thick slices as close to the pit as possible. Scoop out the flesh and chop coarsely. Cut off any flesh adhering to the pit.
2 Peel the kiwi with a sharp knife and chop the flesh.
3 Put the mango, kiwi, pineapple juice, and mint leaves into a food processor or blender and process until thoroughly combined. Pour into chilled glasses and serve.

12 RHUBARB

Rhubarb has been used as a laxative for thousands of years to prevent the build up of aging toxins that can make you feel sluggish and your skin look dull.

Rhubarb roots and stems are rich in anthraquinones. These substances are also found in senna, aloe, and cascara—plants all used in herbal medicine as natural laxatives. Preparations made from these plants are sometimes harsh on the digestive tract, however, which makes dietary sources, such as rhubarb, preferable. As part of a high-fiber diet, rhubarb will help bowel function by toning the muscle of the digestive tract wall and ensure the removal of aging toxic waste without dehydrating or damaging the digestive system. Traditionally, rhubarb has been used to promote skin health and maintain a youthful appearance by this route of cleaning the body and your detoxification pathways from the inside.

- Modulates inflammatory responses, helping restore balance to the immune system and prevent aging diseases.
- Removes excess fats from the bloodstream, helping the circulation deliver revitalizing oxygen and nutrients to the cells.
- Good source of vitamin K, needed for youthful bone health.

Practical tips:
Rhubarb tastes extremely tart on its own so always needs sweetening. Although this can have the effect of negating its healthy properties, honey or fruit juice will minimize the damage. Getting used to the tartness of rhubarb as an aspect of its distinctive flavor also reduces the temptation to oversweeten.

....

DID YOU KNOW?

Rhubarb has been used for thousands of years by the Chinese for digestive and kidney health—both vital body systems for retaining youth—and is also mentioned in medieval European and Arabic medical texts.

....

MAJOR NUTRIENTS PER ¾ CUP SLICED RHUBARB

Calories	21
Total fat	0.2 g
Protein	0.9 g
Carbohydrate	4.54 g
Fiber	1.8 g
Vitamin C	8 mg
Calcium	86 mg
Potassium	288 mg
Vitamin K	29.3 mcg

Sweet and sour fruit compote

SERVES 4

1 lb 7 oz/650 g rhubarb, cut
   into 1-inch/2.5-cm pieces
juice of 2 oranges
5 tbsp good-quality honey
scant 2 cups strawberries

Method

1 Put the rhubarb in a saucepan, add the orange juice and honey, and bring to a boil, stirring gently. Reduce the heat and simmer, stirring occasionally, for 5 minutes.

2 Meanwhile, hull the strawberries and halve any large ones. Add them to the pan and simmer for an additional 5 minutes.

3 Divide the warm compote among individual serving bowls and serve immediately or let cool to room temperature.

13

PURPLE GRAPES

Purple grape varieties are one of the healthiest fruits you can eat and offer potent antiaging skin and heart nutrients.

Purple grape skins and seeds are the best source we have of resveratrol, a valuable bioflavonoid (plant chemical), also found in peanuts and red wine. Since the fruit is eaten whole with its skin, the useful fruit fiber is also left intact. Purple grapes rank with blueberries and blackberries as plentiful sources of proanthocyanidins, found in the red/blue pigmentation of their skin, along with another antioxidant, ellagic acid, which further promotes rejuvenating detoxification. Purple grapes support heart health by protecting "bad" LDL cholesterol (which if damaged can cause harm to arteries), and by helping to reduce high levels of the substance homocysteine, both of which are major contributing factors to heart disease.

- Contain malic acid, which assists in energy production to revitalize cells and repair damage, helping you to maintain a youthful appearance.
- Grape seeds contain oils that are potent natural antibiotics, and that work hard to protect the structure of skin and veins.
- Contain lignans that may help prevent breast cancer.

Practical tips:

Choose fruit that is firmly attached to the stem. Because grapes are high in sucrose, red grape juice is extremely sugary, and this sugar is released into the bloodstream rapidly. Stick to the whole fruit, which contains fiber, too.

DID YOU KNOW?

A bacterium found on the skin of grapes was one of the earliest cultivated micro-organisms. It was used for the fermentation of wine in ancient cultures.

MAJOR NUTRIENTS PER ⅔ CUP PURPLE GRAPES

Calories	69
Total fat	0.16 g
Protein	0.72 g
Carbohydrate	18.1 g
Fiber	0.9 g
Vitamin C	10.8 mg
Potassium	191 mg

Grape, celery, and pecan salad

SERVES 4

2 Boston lettuces, washed
6 celery stalks, chopped
2 cups purple seedless grapes,
    halved if large
heaping ¾ cup shelled pecans
8–10 sprigs watercress,
    for garnishing

Dressing

3 tbsp extra virgin olive oil
½ tbsp red wine vinegar
½ tbsp balsamic vinegar
salt and pepper

Method

1 Trim the root ends off the lettuce and discard any outer damaged leaves. Halve each lettuce lengthwise. Remove 6 whole leaves from the outsides of each lettuce and arrange 3 on each plate. Slice the remaining lettuce and add to the plates.

2 Sprinkle over the chopped celery, grapes, and pecans.

3 To make the dressing, blend together the oil, vinegars, and seasoning in a small bowl and sprinkle over the salads. Garnish with watercress to serve.

14 CURRANTS

Both red currants and black currants are extremely high in vitamin C. Their colors reflect the different combinations of youth-enhancing antioxidants they contain.

Red currants and black currants are even higher on the ORAC index than strawberries and raspberries. This means that they are high in antioxidant phytochemicals, such as vitamin C and proanthocyanidins, which are essential for keeping your hair and skin looking healthy and youthful. They also inhibit the inflammatory mechanisms that may lead to heart disease, Alzheimer's, cancer, and osteoporosis as you grow older. Currants are good sources of minerals for bone health; alkalizing potassium, for example, supports bone regeneration and neutralizes bone-depleting metabolic salts.

- Good source of vitamin B_5, essential for humans to make energy from plant foods for repair and renewal, to keep us looking and feeling young and full of vitality.
- Vitamin B_5 and vitamin C support adrenal function and so help us cope with stressful situations and protect us from aging.
- Iron helps in the production of the mood-balancing neurotransmitter serotonin, which supports a positive outlook and healthy sleep patterns for rejuvenation.

Practical tips:
The astringent flavor of red currants and black currants often forms the basis of sauces that complement meat dishes and desserts. These berries freeze well and, once frozen, you can simply shake them to remove from the stems.

DID YOU KNOW?

Because the European currant is a host to white pine blister rust, a disease that affects the white pine, some states ban growing this fruit, which is why it can be difficult to find fresh.

MAJOR NUTRIENTS PER 1 CUP CURRANTS

Calories	63
Total fat	0.4 g
Protein	1.4 g
Carbohydrate	15.4 g
Vitamin C	181 mg
Vitamin B_5	0.4 mg
Potassium	322 mg
Phosphorus	59 mg
Iron	1.5 mg

Red currant and peach smoothie

SERVES 2

2 large ripe peaches
heaping ¾ cup red currants
heaping ¾ cup ice-cold water
1–2 tbsp good-quality honey

Method

1 Halve the peaches and discard the pits. Coarsely chop and put into a blender.

2 Keep 2 stems of red currants whole for decoration and strip the rest off their stalks into the blender. Add the water and honey and blend until smooth.

3 Pour into glasses and decorate with the remaining red currant sprigs.

15

TAMARIND

Intensely sweet and sour in taste, tamarind is a highly recommended kitchen remedy, long valued for its cleansing, antiaging effects.

Traditionally used as an antimalarial and antiseptic preparation, recent studies have shown that tamarind is an effective antibacterial agent against microbes, such as salmonella and staphylococcus, which can weaken the immune system. As with all bitter foods, it helps stimulate gastric juices and bile flow, facilitating full digestion, nutrient absorption, and the removal of toxins, which damage the body and cause disease and premature aging. If eaten in larger quantities, tamarind is a laxative.

- Its dark color indicates a wealth of antioxidant carotenoids, which protect against the ravages of pollution and stress.
- Has natural preservative qualities when added to food, preventing aging damage from bacterial infection.
- Can be applied to the skin to ease inflammation and limit scar damage, helping you to maintain a youthful appearance.

Practical tips:
Tamarind paste is widely available and makes a useful condiment for the kitchen pantry. In cooking, it can replace yeast extracts, which can exacerbate digestive problems, and it doesn't contain the high salt content of soy sauce. A little-known ingredient in popular condiments, such as Worcestershire sauce, tamarind will also lift the taste of vegetables in stir-fries.

DID YOU KNOW?

Tamarind has been used extensively in the traditional medicines of Asia, Africa, South America, and Iran (formerly Persia). Its name comes from the Persian, meaning "Hindu date."

MAJOR NUTRIENTS PER ¾ CUP TAMARIND PULP

Calories	239
Total fat	0.6 g
Protein	2.8 g
Carbohydrate	62.5 g
Fiber	5.1 g
Vitamin C	3.5 mg
Potassium	628 mg
Magnesium	92 mg
Calcium	74 mg

Tamarind relish

MAKES ABOUT 1 CUP

generous ¾ cup chopped
   tamarind pulp
scant 2 cups water
½ Thai chile, or to taste, seeded
   and chopped
heaping ¼ cup light brown sugar,
   or to taste
½ tsp salt, or to taste

Method

1 Put the tamarind and water in a heavy-bottom saucepan over high heat and bring to a boil. Reduce the heat to the lowest setting and simmer for 25 minutes, or until tender, stirring occasionally to break up the tamarind pulp.

2 Put the tamarind pulp into a strainer, rinse out the pan, and use a wooden spoon to push the pulp back into the pan.

3 Stir in the chile, sugar, and salt and continue simmering for an additional 10 minutes, or until the desired consistency is reached. Let cool slightly, then stir in extra sugar or salt to taste.

4 Let cool completely, then cover tightly. It will keep for up to 3 days in the refrigerator, or can be frozen.

VEGETABLES

Vegetables are the most important part of any diet. These are the mineral- and vitamin-rich leaves, roots, and stalks that are vital to the health of your body. You need a variety of different colored vegetables to keep your body youthful and should aim high: five to eight portions a day proves truly rejuvenating.

(S) Skin, hair, and nails

(M) Mobility and strength

(D) Digestive/detoxification health

(B) Brain health

(H) Heart health

(I) Immunity-supporting antioxidant

16 BELL PEPPERS

All members of the capsicum family, which includes chile and paprika, have fantastic youth-preserving benefits, and are especially good for the heart and skin.

The color of red bell peppers comes from the antioxidant carotenoid lycopene, just one of the nutrients that distinguishes them from green bell peppers. They also have twice the vitamin C and around nine times the carotene as their green counterpart. As part of the youth-preserving Mediterranean diet, red bell peppers contribute to heart health, because their high levels of antioxidants keep the arteries in good condition. The vitamin B_6 and folate present also help to reduce levels of homocysteine, a substance we produce naturally but that is linked to heart disease and dementia if levels become high.

- Vitamin A stops the damage to skin from UV light that can be seen as wrinkles and age spots.
- Contain vitamin C and vitamin B_6, which is needed to make stomach acid, vital for killing off harmful bacteria before it reaches the intestine.
- Contain folate, needed for cell growth and skin renewal to keep you looking young.

Practical tip:
A bell pepper should feel weighty and have a healthy green stem. The skin should be smooth, firm, and wrinkle-free. Avoid peppers with indents or black spots. Store, unwashed, in a plastic bag in the refrigerator for up to a week. Fat-soluble carotenoids need oil to carry them into the body, so eating red bell peppers with olive oil will double their health value and optimize their absorption.

DID YOU KNOW?
In Central and South America people eat an average of about ¼ cup of chopped bell peppers a day. Research suggests that a daily intake of bell peppers may help prevent the formation of cancer cells.

MAJOR NUTRIENTS PER MEDIUM-SIZE RED BELL PEPPER

Calories	37
Total fat	0.36 g
Protein	1.18 g
Carbohydrate	7.18 g
Fiber	2.5 g
Vitamin A	6,681 IU
Vitamin C	222 mg
Vitamin B_6	0.35 mg
Folate	25.7 mcg

Stuffed red bell peppers with basil

SERVES 4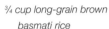

¾ cup long-grain brown
   basmati rice

4 large red bell peppers

2 tbsp olive oil

1 garlic clove, chopped

4 shallots, chopped

1 celery stalk, chopped

3 tbsp chopped walnuts

2 tomatoes, peeled and chopped

1 tbsp lemon juice

heaping ⅓ cup raisins

4 tbsp freshly grated cheddar
   cheese (optional)

2 tbsp chopped
   fresh basil

salt and pepper

Method

1 Preheat the oven to 350ºF/
180ºC. Cook the rice in a
saucepan of lightly salted
boiling water for 35 minutes.
Drain, rinse under cold running
water, then drain again.

2 Meanwhile, using a sharp
knife, cut the tops off the
bell peppers and set aside.
Remove the seeds and white
cores, then blanch the bell

peppers and reserved tops in
boiling water for 2 minutes.
Remove from the heat and
drain well.

3 Heat half the oil in a large
skillet. Add the garlic and
shallots and cook, stirring,
for 3 minutes. Add the celery,
walnuts, tomatoes, lemon
juice, and raisins and cook
for an additional 5 minutes.
Remove from the heat and stir
in the rice, cheese (if using),
chopped basil, and seasoning.

4 Stuff the bell peppers with
the rice mixture and arrange
them in a baking dish. Place
the tops on the bell peppers,
drizzle over the remaining oil,
loosely cover with foil, and
bake in the preheated oven for
45 minutes. Remove from the
oven and serve.

17

SPINACH

Spinach contains many minerals, including magnesium, low levels of which can cause anxiety and insomnia, both well known factors in premature aging.

As a dark green leaf, spinach contains high levels of chlorophyll, which is both alkalizing and cleansing when eaten. The rich color of the spinach leaf is also made up of different colored carotenoids, antioxidant chemicals that protect the plant from UV damage. The darker the leaf, the more of these nutrients it contains, and the more protection it can give you from sun damage to your skin and free radical damage inside the body that can lead to aging inflammatory conditions.

- Contains the brain-cell-supporting substances alpha lipoic acid and glutathione to help retain youthful brain function.
- Source of folate, needed for cell growth, energy, and renewal.
- Contains good amounts of all essential amino acids, crucial for bone and muscle repair, and so maintaining strength and agility.
- Contains good levels of iron, which helps distribute oxygen around the body to replenish cells and keep them as new.

Practical tips:
Steam spinach rather than boil it as this will preserve the folate, whereas boiling for just 4 minutes can halve its content. As with most plant sources, you need vitamin C in order to absorb the bound form of iron in spinach, so eat with the high vitamin C food sources in this book, such as broccoli or red bell pepper.

DID YOU KNOW?

Like cheese, chocolate, and wine, spinach contains the chemical tyramine, which increases the release of stimulating brain chemicals. If you don't sleep well, avoid these foods close to bedtime.

MAJOR NUTRIENTS PER 3⅓ CUPS SPINACH

Calories	23
Total fat	0.4 g
Protein	2.2 g
Carbohydrate	3.6 g
Fiber	2.2 g
Vitamin C	28 mg
Vitamin A	9,377 IU
Beta-carotene	5,626 mcg
Vitamin E	2.03 mg
Vitamin K	483 mg
Folate	194 mg
Calcium	99 mg
Magnesium	79 mg
Iron	2.71 mg

Chunky potato and spinach curry

SERVES 4

4 tomatoes

2 tbsp peanut or light olive oil

2 onions, cut into thick wedges

1-inch/2.5-cm piece fresh ginger,
  peeled and finely chopped

1 garlic clove, chopped

2 tbsp ground coriander

3 medium potatoes, peeled and
  cut into chunks

2½ cups low-salt
  vegetable stock

1 tbsp red curry paste

8 oz/225 g spinach leaves

cooked brown basmati rice,
  for serving (optional)

Method

1 Put the tomatoes in a heatproof bowl and cover with boiling water. Let stand for 1 minute, then plunge into cold water and peel off the skins. Cut each tomato into quarters and remove and discard the seeds and central core. Set aside.

2 Heat the oil in a preheated wok, add the onions, ginger, and garlic and stir-fry over medium–high heat for 2–3 minutes, until starting to soften. Add the coriander and potatoes and stir-fry for 2–3 minutes. Add the stock and curry paste and bring to a boil, stirring occasionally. Reduce the heat and simmer gently for 10–15 minutes, until the potatoes are tender.

3 Add the spinach and the tomato quarters and cook, stirring, for 1 minute, or until the spinach has wilted. Serve with rice, if using.

18

GARLIC

Garlic's traditional use as a medicinal plant is due to its various sulfur compounds, which work to detoxify, cleanse, and repair cells to help you look and feel young.

Garlic is naturally antibacterial, antiparasitic, and antifungal. Use it regularly in cooking to keep the digestive tract clean, support the immune system, and ward off a whole host of infections and conditions that can lead to premature aging. Its ability to kill harmful organisms was recognized during World Wars I and II, when it was used as an antiseptic. Garlic's ability to thin the blood is so strong that a large amount in the diet is dangerous if taken with blood-thinning drugs, such as warfarin. This potency also makes garlic a powerful defense against atherosclerosis and coronary artery disease. As little as one clove a day is effective at lowering blood pressure and regulating cholesterol levels, as well as supporting the skin-nourishing effects of good circulation.

- Contains the prebiotic fiber inulin, which feeds beneficial digestive tract bacteria, aiding digestion and detoxification.
- Sulfur content helps remove harmful and aging toxic metals, such as lead and mercury.
- Traditionally associated with youthful vitality and to ward off the illnesses that contribute to premature aging.

Practical tips:
Cooking garlic reduces its potency, whereas eating it raw is a good all-round home remedy. Chopping, crushing, or chewing releases the chemical allicin, which has antibacterial and antifungal properties, and is also responsible for the hot taste.

DID YOU KNOW?

One of the oldest flavorings used in cooking, garlic was served on bread to help sustain the workers building the pyramids. Purple heads of garlic with around 45 cloves have been found in Egyptian tombs.

MAJOR NUTRIENTS PER 2 GARLIC CLOVES

Calories	8
Total fat	0.3 g
Protein	0.38 g
Carbohydrate	0.99 g
Fiber	0.2 g
Vitamin C	0.9 mg
Potassium	24 mg

Aioli

SERVES 4

3 large garlic cloves, finely chopped
2 egg yolks
1 cup extra virgin olive oil
1 tbsp lemon juice
1 tbsp lime juice
1 tbsp Dijon mustard
1 tbsp chopped fresh tarragon
salt and pepper
1 fresh tarragon sprig, for
* garnishing*

Method

1 Ensure that all the ingredients are at room temperature. Place the garlic and egg yolks in a food processor and process until well blended.

2 With the motor running, pour in the oil, teaspoon by teaspoon, through the feeder tube until the mixture starts to thicken, then pour in the remaining oil in a thin stream until a thick mayonnaise forms. It is essential to add oil slowly to the egg yolks to prevent them from curdling until between one-third and one-half has been fully incorporated. If the mixture does curdle, add it, a little at a time, to another egg yolk, whisking constantly, then return it to the food processor, and gradually add the remaining oil with the motor running all the time.

3 Add the lemon and lime juices, mustard, and tarragon, and season with salt and pepper to taste. Blend until smooth, then transfer the aioli to a nonmetallic bowl. Garnish with a tarragon sprig.

4 Cover with plastic wrap and chill until required.

19

CELERY

Wild celery has been used medicinally in many cultures for hundreds of years. Its calming effect helps prevent insomnia and anxiety, which are both highly aging.

Research into celery has shown resoundingly good results when it comes to lowering blood pressure. Just four stalks a day have proved to be effective. This is because the chemicals apigenin and phthalide expand the blood vessels, which prompts a lowering of pressure overall. This action also activates the calming part of the nervous system, creating a soothing effect and relieving stress. Celery contains tryptophan, a protein that we use to make the sleep- and mood-regulating hormone serotonin, which adds to its power as an insomnia and anxiety reliever, both of which conditions are known to age us prematurely.

- Commonly used in weight-loss programs as the bulky fiber requires energy to digest, leaving very few calories remaining.
- Potassium also helps to shed excess fluid to help you retain a youthful body shape and prevent cellulite.
- Regulates appetite and helps you maintain an ideal weight.
- High levels of potassium and vitamin C keep the heart young.

Practical tips:
Celery is delicious either raw or cooked, and is the basis of most stocks. Celery seeds are dried and ground to make celery salt, a low-sodium flavoring used in cocktails.

DID YOU KNOW?

The Romans wore celery wreaths around their heads to "protect" them from hangovers. Today, athletes often use celery juice as a post-training recovery drink as it perfectly rehydrates and helps restore tired muscles.

MAJOR NUTRIENTS PER 1 CUP CHOPPED CELERY

Calories	16
Total fat	0.17 g
Protein	0.69 g
Carbohydrate	2.97 g
Fiber	1.6 g
Vitamin C	3.1 mg
Vitamin B_3	0.32 mg
Vitamin B_5	0.25 mg
Folate	36 mg
Calcium	40 mg
Magnesium	11 mg
Potassium	260 mg

Carrot, celery, and apple soup

SERVES 4

2 lb/900 g carrots, finely diced
1 onion, chopped
3 celery stalks, diced
4 cups low-salt vegetable stock
2 medium apples, plus 1
    for garnishing
2 tbsp tomato paste
1 bay leaf
juice of ¼ large lemon
salt and pepper
shredded celery leaves,
    for garnishing

Method

1   Place the carrots, onion, and celery in a large saucepan and add the vegetable stock. Bring to a boil, reduce the heat, cover, and simmer for 10 minutes.

2   Meanwhile, peel, core, and dice 2 of the apples. Add the diced apple, tomato paste, and bay leaf to the saucepan and bring to a boil over medium heat. Reduce the heat, partially cover, and simmer for 20 minutes. Remove and discard the bay leaf.

3   Meanwhile, wash and core the remaining apple and cut into thin slices, without peeling. Place the apple slices in a small saucepan and squeeze over the lemon juice. Heat the apple slices gently and simmer for 1–2 minutes, or until the apple is tender. Drain the apple slices and set aside until required.

4   Place the carrot-and-apple mixture in a food processor or blender and process until smooth. Return the soup to the rinsed-out saucepan, reheat gently, if necessary, and season with salt and pepper to taste. Ladle the soup into 4 warmed bowls, top with the reserved apple slices and shredded celery leaves, and serve immediately.

20 CARROTS

The bright orange color of carrots signifies their high beta- and alpha-carotene levels. This gives them the ability to rejuvenate your skin and other organs.

As one of the root vegetables you can eat raw, carrots are a more nutritious and natural food than vegetables you have to cook, such as potatoes and parsnips. However, carrots do benefit from slight cooking as it helps them release their antioxidant carotenoids. You also need oil to absorb these fat-soluble nutrients. A raw carrot will yield 3 percent beta-carotene, which can increase to 39 percent if steamed, juiced, or cooked in oil. Your body converts beta-carotene into vitamin A, which is needed for healthy eyesight and to aid detoxification. Carrots are also high in vitamin A that doesn't need converting, so they do their utmost to keep you youthful.

- A newly discovered chemical in carrots called falcarinol has been shown to have strong skin-protecting antioxidant activity.
- The fiber in carrots, pectin, detoxifies heavy metals, such as lead and cadmium and other aging toxins.
- Source of the flavonoid rutin, which helps prevent unsightly varicose veins, high blood pressure, and heart disease.

Practical tips:
Cooking carrots lightly by stir-frying or steaming, so they are still slightly crunchy, is the healthiest option, but eating them raw as snacks or grated in salads provides good cleansing fiber. Add flax oil to carrot juice to release the beta-carotene.

DID YOU KNOW?

Before the Dutch bred the sweet, orange carrot that we know today, the carrot was a bitter, lumpy, purple thing, the leafy tops of which were used as decoration on Elizabethan hats.

MAJOR NUTRIENTS PER ¾ CUP CHOPPED CARROTS

Calories	41
Total fat	0.24 g
Protein	0.93 g
Carbohydrate	9.58 g
Fiber	2.8 g
Vitamin C	5.9 mg
Vitamin A	16,706 IU
Potassium	320 mg
Beta-carotene	8,285 mg
Alpha-carotene	3,477 mg

Roasted carrot pâté with feta

SERVES 4–6

8 medium carrots, about
  1 lb 2 oz/500 g, peeled
  and thickly sliced
heaping ⅓ cup extra virgin olive oil
2 tsp cumin seeds, toasted
  and ground
¾ cup crumbled, drained
  feta cheese or fresh firm
  goat cheese
salt and pepper
1 small bunch of fresh cilantro,
  finely chopped, for garnishing

Method

1 Preheat the oven to 400°F/200°C. Put the carrots in an ovenproof dish, pour over the oil, and cover the dish with foil. Bake in the preheated oven for about 25 minutes.

2 Meanwhile, heat a dry, heavy-bottom skillet over medium–high heat. Add the cumin seeds and cook for 3–4 minutes, tossing the seeds frequently, until lightly toasted and fragrant. Let cool, then grind using a mortar and pestle or an electric grinder, to form a coarse powder.

3 Remove the foil from the ovenproof dish, toss in the ground cumin seeds, and bake for an additional 15 minutes, or until tender.

4 Mash the carrots with a fork, combining them with the oil in the dish, or process them to a paste in a blender or food processor. Season with salt and pepper to taste and spoon into a serving dish. Scatter the crumbled feta cheese over the top and garnish with the cilantro. Serve warm or at room temperature.

21

SQUASH

Squash contains coumarins, chemicals that are anti-inflammatory, antioxidant, and antibacterial, which prevents damage to the skin, joints, brain, and heart.

Coumarins are also important in protecting and supporting heart function, balancing heart rhythm, and regulating blood pressure to keep you healthy and feeling young. Squash is also a good source of the trace mineral manganese, which is needed in small amounts to get the best out of fats and proteins, create bone, renew skin, absorb calcium, regulate sex hormones, balance blood sugar, and create new DNA so that the body is able to heal. Manganese is a crucial component in superoxide dismutase (SOD), an antioxidant that is present in all cells to protect them from aging.

- Contains vitamins A and C, antioxidants that destroy harmful free radical molecules and so protect us from heat and light damage, helping the skin maintain a youthful appearance.
- Potassium, magnesium, and manganese help prevent the inflammation linked to age-related diseases.
- Potassium and magnesium also help regulate heart function and keep blood pressure low.

Practical tips:
A squash should feel heavy for its size, or it will have dry and mealy flesh. Choose ones with shiny skins and no pockmarks or bruises. Keep in a plastic bag in the refrigerator for up to a week. To make a tasty filler for wraps, cut in half, drizzle with olive oil, and bake in a preheated oven (400°F/200°C) for 20 minutes. Scoop out the cooked flesh and add to goat cheese and watercress.

DID YOU KNOW?

Squashes originate from South America and are botanically related to melons and cucumbers. In Australia, butternut squash is used in the same way as pumpkin, to which it is closely related.

MAJOR NUTRIENTS PER ¾ CUP CUBED SQUASH

Calories	45
Total fat	0.1 g
Protein	1 g
Carbohydrate	11.69 g
Fiber	2 g
Vitamin C	21 mg
Vitamin A	10,630 IU
Calcium	34 mg
Magnesium	26 mcg
Potassium	352 mcg
Manganese	0.2 mcg

Spinach and squash bake

SERVES 4

2 cups peeled, seeded, and
   cubed squash
2 small red onions, each cut into
   8 segments
2 tsp olive oil
4¼ oz/120 g baby spinach leaves
2 tbsp whole wheat breadcrumbs
pepper

White sauce

heaping 1 cup milk or soy milk
2 tsp cornstarch
1 tsp dry mustard
1 small onion
2 small bay leaves
4 tsp grated Parmesan or
   Pecorino cheese (optional)

Method

1 Preheat the oven to 400°F/
   200°C and warm an ovenproof
   serving dish.

2 Arrange the prepared squash
   and onion on a nonstick baking
   sheet and coat with the oil and
   plenty of black pepper. Bake for
   20 minutes, turning once.

3 To make the sauce, put the
   milk into a small nonstick
   saucepan with the cornstarch,
   mustard, onion, and bay
   leaves. Whisk over medium
   heat until thick. Remove from
   the heat, discard the onion
   and bay leaves, and stir in the

cheese, if using. Set aside,
stirring occasionally to prevent
a skin from forming.

4 When the squash is nearly
   cooked, put the spinach
   in a large saucepan with 2
   tablespoons of water and stir
   over medium heat for 2–3
   minutes or until just wilted.

5 Put half the squash mixture in
   the warmed ovenproof dish
   and top with half the spinach.
   Repeat the layers. Pour over
   the white sauce and sprinkle
   over the breadcrumbs.

6 Transfer to the oven and cook
   for 15–20 minutes.

22

BRUSSELS SPROUTS

Brussels sprouts contain a substance called sinigrin that works as a powerful antioxidant in the liver, detoxifying and eliminating harmful, aging substances.

All members of the cruciferous family, which includes cabbage, cauliflower, broccoli, and kale as well as Brussels sprouts, contain sulfurous chemicals, called glucosinolates, which have been shown to reduce tumors and the incidence of cancer, particularly estrogen-related cancers, such as breast and prostate. Sulforaphane, a potent type of glucosinolate in these vegetables, is known to boost the body's own cleansing and detoxification enzymes, which keep our systems young and free of toxins. Sulforaphane is formed when cruciferous vegetables are chopped or chewed.

- Sulfur compounds combined with the high fiber content reduce "bad" LDL cholesterol and remove aging toxins.
- Thirty-one percent of the calories in Brussels sprouts come from protein, making them fabulous for keeping skin and bone rejuvenated and young.
- Good source of vitamins A, C, and E and lutein, which adds to this vegetable's antiaging, anticancer properties.

Practical tip:
Brussels sprouts only need 6–7 minutes' steaming or boiling. Any longer and the sulfurous smell will be released. Cutting the stem right off up to the beginning of the leaves and then scoring two lines deep into the base to form a cross helps them cook more thoroughly in this short time.

DID YOU KNOW?

Most Brussels sprouts are grown in California, where as much as 85 percent are destined for frozen food departments.

MAJOR NUTRIENTS PER 3½ oz/100 g BRUSSELS SPROUTS

Calories	43
Total fat	0.3 g
Protein	3.38 g
Carbohydrate	8.95 g
Fiber	3.8 g
Vitamin C	85 mg
Vitamin A	754 IU
Vitamin E	0.88 mg
Folate	61 mcg
Iron	1.4 mg
Lutein/Zeaxanthin	1,590 mcg

Sprouts with garlic and almonds

SERVES 4

24–32 Brussels sprouts,
    depending on size
1 tbsp olive oil
3 garlic cloves, finely chopped
2 tbsp low-salt vegetable stock
scant ¾ cup slivered almonds
½ tsp grated nutmeg
heaping ⅓ cup plain live yogurt
salt and pepper

Method

1 Wash the sprouts, remove any yellowing leaves and trim the bases. Slice in half. Bring a saucepan of water to a boil and blanch or steam the sprouts for 2 minutes. Drain and dry thoroughly in a clean dish towel or paper towels.

2 Heat the oil in a skillet, add the sprouts, and stir well over medium–high heat for 1 minute, or until just tinged golden brown. Add the garlic and cook for an additional 1 minute, stirring once or twice. Add the stock, cover, turn the heat down to medium, and cook for 2 minutes, or until tender but still with a bite.

3 Add the almonds, nutmeg, yogurt, salt, and pepper and stir gently to combine. Heat through for 1 minute before serving.

23 ONIONS

Onions have long been valued for their anti-inflammatory and healing properties, and are closely associated with antiaging and longevity.

Onions and their relatives in the allium family, garlic and leeks, contain sulfur compounds called allyl sulfides, which have been shown to help lower blood pressure and discourage the growth of tumors. Like apples and green tea, onions are also high in a plant chemical called quercetin, which is an excellent antioxidant. Quercetin is also an antihistamine and has anti-inflammatory properties. It blocks an enzyme in the body that can cause the accumulation of sorbitol, a sugar that at high levels is associated with damage to the eyes, kidneys, and nerves.

- Contain vitamin C, vitamin B_6, calcium, potassium, and phosphorus, which all play a role in keeping your heart healthy.
- Phosphorus content draws calcium into new bone growth, keeping the body young and strong.
- Also shown to destroy osteoclasts, cells that break down bone, thereby reducing the risk of osteoporosis.

Practical tips:
There are numerous varieties of onion, from the larger, more strongly sulfuric white types that are so good for cooking, to the red or smaller, sweeter varieties, such as shallots. Try eating shallots raw to get the full benefit of their phytochemicals. Onions are also good roasted whole in olive oil, with rosemary and whole cloves of garlic. Opt for a strong onion on occasion; the stronger the taste, the more cancer-fighting flavonoids the onion contains.

DID YOU KNOW?

Because they have particularly large and visible cellulose structures, onions are routinely placed under school microscopes as an example of plant cells.

MAJOR NUTRIENTS PER ⅔ CUP CHOPPED ONION

Calories	40
Total fat	0.1 g
Protein	1.1 g
Carbohydrate	9.34 g
Fiber	1.7 g
Vitamin C	7.4 mg
Vitamin B_6	0.12 mg
Potassium	146 mg
Phosphorus	29 mg
Calcium	23 mg

Chile and onion salsa

MAKES ABOUT 1 CUP

1–2 fresh green chiles, finely
   chopped (seeded, if you like)

1 small Thai chile, finely chopped
   (seeded, if you like)

1 tbsp cider vinegar

2 white onions, finely chopped

2 tbsp fresh lemon juice

1 tbsp good-quality honey

3 tbsp chopped fresh cilantro,
   mint, or parsley, or a
   combination of herbs

salt

chile flower, for garnishing

Method

1 To make the chile flower garnish, use a sharp knife to make several
  cuts lengthwise along the chile, keeping the stem end intact. Put
  the chile in a bowl of iced water and let stand for 25–30 minutes,
  or until the cut edges have spread out to form a flower shape.

2 Put the chopped chiles in a small nonmetallic bowl with the vinegar,
  stir, and then drain. Return the chiles to the bowl and stir in the
  onions, lemon juice, honey, and herbs, then add salt to taste.

3 Let the salsa stand at room temperature or cover and chill for
  15 minutes. Garnish with the chile flower before serving.

24 WATERCRESS

Watercress stimulates bile flow in the liver, promoting detoxification and digestion, to remove aging components and absorb revitalizing nutrients.

Watercress contains isothiocyanates, a superior type of detoxifying, cancer-preventing sulfur compound. Sulfur is the key to watercress's potency. It is vital for detoxifying alcohol in the system, to achieve balance in the body's sex hormones, and helps restore vigor in both women and men. It may also help prevent hormone-related cancers, and aids circulation, taking nutrients and oxygen to wherever they are needed in the body to promote fresh, glowing skin. It is important in healing, too, and is used with vitamin C to make collagen, ensuring that the skin stays firm and wrinkle-free, and the muscles and bones are strong.

- Contains a large amount of folate, which promotes skin renewal. The darker the leaf, the more folate it contains.
- Contains antioxidant carotenoids, which protect the leaf from UV damage and in turn protect us from premature aging and skin damage caused by sunlight.
- High in the antioxidant vitamins A, C, and E, which help prevent wrinkles, age spots, and skin damage.
- High iodine content regulates metabolism and helps you maintain a healthy, youthful weight.

Practical tips:
Choose dark green leaves with no yellowing parts. Buy bunched, uncovered watercress where possible rather than the bagged variety and eat immediately.

DID YOU KNOW?

Watercress is botanically related to mustard. The characteristic bitter, peppery taste of the watercress leaf only develops when the plant starts flowering.

MAJOR NUTRIENTS PER 10 SPRIGS WATERCRESS

Calories	3
Total fat	Trace
Protein	0.6 g
Carbohydrate	0.3 g
Fiber	Trace
Vitamin A	798 IU
Vitamin C	11 mg
Vitamin E	0.25 mg
Vitman K	62 mcg
Folate	2.25 mg
Iron	0.06 mg
Beta-carotene	478 mcg
Lutein/Zeaxanthin	1,442 mcg

Watercress soup

SERVES 4

2 bunches watercress,
   thoroughly cleaned
3 tbsp butter
2 onions, chopped
1½ cups peeled and coarsely
   chopped potatoes
8 cups low-salt vegetable stock
   or water
whole nutmeg, for grating
salt and pepper
live Greek-style yogurt and extra
   virgin olive oil, for serving

Method

1 Remove the leaves from the stalks of the watercress and keep on one side. Coarsely chop the stalks.

2 Melt the butter in a large saucepan over medium heat, add the onions, and cook for 4–5 minutes, until soft. Do not brown.

3 Add the potatoes to the saucepan and mix well with the onions. Add the watercress stalks and the stock.

4 Bring to a boil, then reduce the heat, cover, and simmer for 15–20 minutes, until the potato is soft.

5 Add the watercress leaves and stir in to heat through. Remove from the heat and use a handheld immersion blender to process the soup until smooth. Alternatively, blend the soup in a blender and return to the rinsed-out saucepan. Reheat and season with salt and pepper to taste, adding a good grating of nutmeg.

6 Serve in warmed bowls topped with a spoonful of yogurt, an extra grating of nutmeg, and a drizzle of olive oil.

25 LEEKS

Members of the health-giving allium family along with garlic and onions, leeks contain sulfur for healthy and youthful skin, bones, and heart.

Leeks contain important substances called saponins, soapy compounds that bind to cholesterol in the bowel, preventing it from being reabsorbed and ensuring that it is excreted. Extensive research has shown that saponins are natural antibiotics, meaning that they reduce our risk of infection and the need for medical antibiotics that can disrupt our beneficial digestive tract flora. They are also potent antioxidants and appear to kill or inhibit cancer cells. They have been shown to be specifically effective at preventing bowel cancer by neutralizing harmful bacteria in the bowel that can become carcinogenic when exposed to bile.

- Contain high levels of the prebiotic fiber that feeds beneficial probiotic fiber in the digestive tract, helping to reduce aging inflammation.
- Sulfur compounds aid detoxification processes to remove toxins from the body before they contribute to aging processes.
- Contain vitamin K, needed for bone renewal.
- Vitamin B_6 and folate are both methylating agents, needed for detoxification and to keep the brain functioning youthfully.

Practical tips:
Leeks can be substituted for onions in most recipes and may be tolerated by those who are sensitive to the higher sulfur content of onions. Be careful when preparing as overcooking leeks can render them an unappetizing mush. They are especially delicious served raw and thinly sliced in salads.

DID YOU KNOW?

The Greek philosopher Aristotle believed that the clear call of the partridge derived from a diet of leeks, while Emperor Nero ate them specifically to improve his singing voice.

MAJOR NUTRIENTS PER MEDIUM-SIZE LEEK

Calories	61
Total fat	0.3 g
Protein	1.5 g
Carbohydrate	2.9 g
Fiber	1.8 g
Vitamin C	12 mg
Vitamin B_6	0.23 mg
Vitamin K	47 mcg
Folate	64 mcg
Calcium	59 mg
Magnesium	28 mg

Leeks with yellow bean sauce

SERVES 6

1 lb/450 g leeks
12 baby corn cobs
6 scallions
3 tbsp peanut oil
2⅓ cups shredded Chinese
    cabbage
4 tbsp yellow bean sauce

Method

1 Using a sharp knife, slice the leeks, halve the baby corn cobs, and thinly slice the scallions.

2 Heat the peanut oil in a large, preheated wok or skillet until it is smoking.

3 Add the leeks, shredded Chinese cabbage, and baby corn to the wok.

4 Stir-fry the vegetables over high heat for about 5 minutes, or until the edges of the vegetables are slightly brown.

5 Add the scallions to the wok, stirring to combine.

6 Add the yellow bean sauce to the wok. Continue to stir-fry the mixture in the wok for an additional 2 minutes, or until the yellow bean sauce is heated through and the vegetables are coated in the sauce.

7 Transfer the stir-fried vegetables and sauce to warmed serving dishes and serve immediately.

26

JERUSALEM ARTICHOKES

These root vegetables are one of our richest sources of the fiber inulin, which supports good digestive health, crucial in the quest to stay young.

The fructose plant fiber inulin is present in more than 36,000 plants world-wide, but it exists in its highest amounts in Jerusalem artichokes. Next down the list is chicory, then garlic and leek. Inulin, usually taken from Jerusalem artichoke and chicory, is now added to many foods because prebiotic fiber is understood to be as important a factor in digestive system health and youthfulness as the probiotic beneficial bacteria that it feeds. For optimal health, about 80 percent of bacteria in our digestive tract should be good, working for our health by forcing out bacteria, viruses, and parasites. Because it is not digested, inulin also cleans out the digestive system as it moves through and picks up aging toxins that need to be excreted.

- High in the B vitamins thiamine (B_1) and niacin (B_3), which make the energy we need to repair cells and stay young.
- Combination of fiber, vitamin C, and potassium helps lower high blood pressure and regulate cholesterol for heart health.
- Source of iron, necessary for transporting oxygen around the body and to rejuvenate all body parts.

Practical tips:
Jerusalem artichokes may be either smooth or knobbly. Avoid any that have started to sprout. Like potatoes, they can be eaten with or without skins, but keeping the skin on will ensure their nutrient value remains intact. Don't overcook or they will become mushy. Their inulin content can cause gas in some people.

DID YOU KNOW?

Neither an artichoke nor from Jerusalem, the Jerusalem artichoke is actually a type of daisy. It tastes similar to artichoke, but the reason for the geographical reference is less clear.

MAJOR NUTRIENTS PER ⅔ CUP SLICED JERUSALEM ARTICHOKES

Calories	73
Total fat	0.01 g
Protein	2 g
Carbohydrate	17.44 g
Fiber	1.6 g
Vitamin C	4 mg
Vitamin B_1	0.2 mg
Vitamin B_3	1.3 mg
Iron	3.4 mg
Potassium	429 mg

Vegetable brochettes with Jerusalem artichoke hummus

SERVES 4

8 shallots, peeled
8 button mushrooms
2 yellow zucchini, cut into rounds
2 red bell peppers, seeded and cut
    into chunks
1 small eggplant, cut into chunks
1 sweet potato, peeled and cut
    into chunks
2 tbsp olive oil
juice of 1 lemon
1 fresh rosemary sprig, leaves
    removed and finely chopped

Hummus

12 oz/350 g Jerusalem artichokes
1 tbsp extra virgin olive oil
1 tbsp butter
¾ cup milk
1¼ cups cooked or canned
    chickpeas, drained and rinsed
1 tsp ground cumin
2 tbsp lemon juice
1 garlic clove, crushed
pepper

Method

1 Presoak 8 wooden skewers
in cold water for 30 minutes,
then drain. Thread an equal
quantity of the vegetables
onto the skewers and put
into a shallow, nonmetallic
dish. Mix the oil, lemon juice,
and rosemary together in a
small bowl and pour over
the skewers. Cover and let
marinate at room temperature
for 30 minutes.

2 Meanwhile, to make the
hummus, put the artichokes
into a large saucepan of
boiling water and cook for
5 minutes, or until tender.
Drain, transfer the artichokes
to a food processor or blender
with the oil, butter, and milk,
and process until smooth.
Add the chickpeas, cumin,
lemon juice, garlic, and
pepper to taste and process
again until smooth. Transfer to
a serving dish.

3 Preheat the broiler to medium.
Lift the brochettes from the
marinade, arrange on the
broiler pan, and cook under
the preheated broiler for
15 minutes, turning frequently,
until the vegetables are soft
and flecked with brown.

4 Serve the brochettes
immediately with the hummus.

27 SAUERKRAUT

Sauerkraut is finely shredded cabbage that has been fermented by health-giving bacteria. It has a long history as a highly nutritious, antiaging food.

Sauerkraut is among many traditional fermented foods associated with a youthful digestive system. This is due to the support these foods give to the 2–3 lb/1–1.5 kg of probiotic bacteria covering the lining of our digestive tract and other mucus membranes, such as the throat. These are our first line of immune defense against bacteria, yeasts, and viruses. They effectively regulate the intestinal environment, sorting out any diarrhea or constipation problems, preventing inflammatory conditions, and by ensuring our immune responses only react to genuine threats and do not overreact to harmless agents, such as food.

- Contains a high amount of glutamine, the amino acid found in muscle that is crucial for youthful movement and strength.
- Includes all the health benefits of the cruciferous cabbage it is made from. Like broccoli and Brussels sprouts, it contains revitalizing and detoxifying sulfur chemicals.
- Sauerkraut juice helps respiration. A good intake of oxygen to replenish body cells is a crucial factor in staying young.

Practical tips:
The lactic acid in sauerkraut can be mildly upsetting for people who are not used to it, but starting with small amounts and building up can help address the bacterial digestive tract imbalance that is the reason for this. Its sourness is then a welcome complement to meat, cheese, and salads.

DID YOU KNOW?

Before the Royal Navy made the change to limes, Captain James Cook took sauerkraut on his sea voyages as a vitamin C-rich preventative to scurvy. The lactic acid bacteria in sauerkraut gives it its distinctive taste.

MAJOR NUTRIENTS PER ½ CUP SAUERKRAUT
(INCLUDING LIQUID)

Calories	19
Total fat	0.14 g
Protein	0.9 g
Carbohydrate	4.3 g
Fiber	2.9 g
Vitamin C	15 mg
Vitamin B$_6$	0.13 mg
Iron	1.5 mg

Sauerkraut salad with chicken

SERVES 4

14 oz/400 g canned sauerkraut,
   drained and rinsed
2 small red apples
1 carrot, cut into thin strips
1 lb/450 g cooked, boneless,
   skinless free-range chicken
   breast

Dressing
heaping ⅓ cup plain live yogurt
1 tsp good-quality honey
salt and pepper

Method

1 Spoon the sauerkraut into a serving dish. Core the apples and chop into small, bite-size pieces, then stir into the sauerkraut.

2 Add the carrot to the sauerkraut, reserving a few strips for garnishing. Slice the chicken breast and stir into the salad.

3 To make the dressing, combine the yogurt with the salt, pepper, and honey in a small bowl. Pour over the salad and toss. Cover and let stand in the refrigerator for 30 minutes, then serve, garnished with a few strips of carrot if liked.

28

PURPLE SPROUTING BROCCOLI

This purple, long-stalked variety of broccoli contains the same health benefits as its stockier cousin, but has the added bonus of antioxidant proanthocyanidins.

The proanthocyanidins, which give purple sprouting broccoli its color, are the same protective polyphenols found in dark red and purple berries that promote circulation and glowing skin, and protect veins and arteries to support heart and brain health. The characteristic taste of cruciferous vegetables comes from sulfurous compounds called isothiocyanates, which have been shown to have a strongly protective effect in people showing a genetic predisposition for lung cancer. Another sulfur compound, sulforaphane, triggers our natural detoxification enzymes.

- Contains the rare vegetable fiber calcium pectate, which holds cholesterol in the liver, limiting its release into the bloodstream.
- Source of the trace mineral chromium, which enables the hormone insulin to move sugar from the bloodstream to cells, so helping prevent adult-onset diabetes.
- Vitamin C and the carotenoids beta-carotene and lutein provide further antioxidant protection for youthful-looking skin.
- Contains vitamin B_5, needed to release energy from the plant foods we eat, encouraging age-defying vigor.

Practical tips:
Cook broccoli only lightly, preferably by steaming, to ensure that it remains slightly crunchy. The sprouting variety has a finer stalk than the fatter vegetable so can be eaten whole. Broccoli works well in stir-fries, or served cold in salads.

DID YOU KNOW?

Although it has only come back into fashion in the last 30 years, purple sprouting broccoli is the most ancient of broccolis, and was cultivated by the Romans.

MAJOR NUTRIENTS PER 3½ oz/100 g PURPLE SPROUTING BROCCOLI

Calories	34
Total fat	0.37 g
Protein	2.82 g
Carbohydrate	6.64 g
Fiber	2.6 g
Vitamin C	89.2 mg
Vitamin B_5	0.57 mg
Calcium	47 mg
Beta-carotene	361 mcg
Lutein/Zeaxanthin	1,121 mcg

Purple sprouting broccoli with garlic and chile

SERVES 4

1 lb 2 oz/500 g purple sprouting
    broccoli
3 tbsp olive oil
2 garlic cloves, finely chopped
1 medium-hot fresh red chile,
    seeded and finely chopped
juice of 1 lime
salt and pepper

Method

1 Trim the broccoli stems as necessary. Bring a saucepan of water to a boil and blanch or steam the stems for 2 minutes. Drain and dry thoroughly in a clean dish towel or paper towels.

2 Heat the olive oil in a skillet over medium heat. Add the broccoli stems and cook for 2 minutes, turning once or twice.

3 Add the garlic and chile to the skillet. Cook for an additional 1 minute, or until the broccoli is just tender.

4 Season with a little salt and plenty of pepper, and stir in the lime juice to serve.

29

SHIITAKE MUSHROOMS

Shiitake are a traditional remedy in their native Japan, Korea, China, and Thailand, where they are prized for their ability to improve vitality and immunity.

Shiitake demonstrate what is known as "immune modulating" properties and are often taken as supplements for this reason. They do not simply boost immunity but regulate it, so that our immune reactions are more appropriate. This has been shown to help reduce sensitivities and intolerances that cause inflammation, bloating, and skin problems, particularly as we age. The mushrooms also directly destroy invading viruses and harmful bacteria and can improve our capacity to fight off these organisms before they take hold, including the powerful flu virus. The substance lentinan is extracted from shiitake as an anticancer treatment, and is used intravenously in some countries.

- Rich source of beta-glucan, which helps the liver recover from aging toxins, such as alcohol.
- Vitamin B_3 helps the body metabolize sugar and so keeps weight from creeping up as we get older.
- Contain the minerals zinc and selenium, which make antioxidant enzymes in the body to keep us young on the inside.

Practical tips:
Shiitake can be bought fresh and dried and both forms are commonly used with miso to make a healthy soup. The drying process brings out the umami taste that is characteristic of Asian cooking, and also makes the proteins slightly easier to assimilate. Fresh shiitake can be used successfully in stir-fries.

DID YOU KNOW?

Shiitake mushrooms were first recorded as a cultivated and medicinal food during the Chinese Song dynasty of AD 960–1127, although some documents mention the uncultivated form as early as AD 199.

MAJOR NUTRIENTS PER 1¾ oz/50 G SHIITAKE MUSHROOMS

Calories	17
Total fat	0.25 g
Protein	1.12 g
Carbohydrate	3.4 g
Fiber	1.3 g
Vitamin B₃	1.9 mg
Selenium	2.9 mg
Zinc	0.51 mg

Fresh shiitake mushroom sushi

MAKES 10 PIECES

scant 1 cup Japanese short-grain
  white rice
heaping ¾ cup water
1 tbsp Japanese soy sauce
  or tamari
10 fresh shiitake mushrooms,
  stems removed
½ sheet toasted nori

For serving

Japanese soy sauce
pickled ginger
wasabi paste

Method

1 To make sushi rice, rinse the rice in several changes of cold water until it runs clear. Put in a saucepan with the measured water and bring to a boil. Reduce the heat to very low and cook until the water has evaporated.

2 Brush the soy sauce on the mushrooms, and cook under a hot broiler for 1–2 minutes on each side, or until tender.

3 Cut the nori into 10 strips about ½ inch/1 cm wide and 3 inches/7.5 cm long.

4 Wet a finger sushi mold. Fill each section with sushi rice, working the rice into the corners without pressing too hard. Press down with the lid, then remove it and turn the neat blocks out onto a cutting board. Repeat so that you have 10 blocks.

5 Alternatively, shape the rice by hand. Take a golfball-size amount of rice in the palm of one hand, then gently press it into an oblong, using your palm and the fingers of your other hand. Repeat to make 10 blocks and place on a cutting board.

6 Place 1 broiled mushroom, skin-side down, on each rice block. Secure with a nori strip, tucking the ends under the rice block. Serve with soy sauce, pickled ginger, and wasabi paste on the side.

30 RADISH

Radishes are among the most nutritious of plant roots, and have traditionally been used to help maintain a youthful appearance and control weight.

Radishes have long been used to treat thyroid conditions. This is because they contain a chemical called raphanin, which, according to researchers, regulates the thyroid gland by tempering its tendency to produce too little or too much thyroid hormone. Low function or hypothyroidism is more common, especially as we age, when the thyroid can slow down and result in weight gain, cold hands, and fatigue. Good levels of the trace mineral molybdenum in radishes also helps balance blood-sugar levels, which again supports the thyroid in its job of managing body weight and energy use.

- The chemical xylogen in radishes reduces infection and inflammation, thereby strengthening your immune system to help prevent disease and premature aging.
- The slightly bitter taste encourages bile flow, helping you digest fats and regulate cholesterol to maintain a trim figure and healthy weight.
- Potassium regulates blood pressure, which keeps your heart healthy and able to pump revitalizing nutrients around your body.

Practical tips:

As well as being a crisp salad vegetable, radishes taste very refreshing in juices. To combat nasal congestion, try processing together six radishes, one cucumber, and one apple. Daikon, also known as winter radish, is a long, white radish used in Asian cooking that can also be eaten raw in thin, long strips in salad.

DID YOU KNOW?

Radishes are used in traditional Chinese medicine to provide kidney, digestive, and liver support and to reduce mucus, sinusitis, and throat problems.

MAJOR NUTRIENTS PER 2 RADISHES

Calories	2
Total fat	0 g
Protein	0.06 g
Carbohydrate	0.30 g
Fiber	0.2 g
Vitamin C	1.4 mg
Folate	2 mcg
Potassium	20 mg
Calcium	2 mg

New potato, radish, and arugula salad

SERVES 4 　(D)(H)(I)

*1 lb 2 oz/500 g new potatoes,
    halved*
8 radishes, thinly sliced
1 small red onion, thinly sliced
1½ cups arugula leaves

Dressing

⅔ cup plain live yogurt
2 tbsp milk
*3 gherkins, drained and finely
    chopped*
2 tbsp chopped fresh dill
salt and pepper

Method

1　Cook the potatoes in a large saucepan of lightly salted boiling
　　water for 12–15 minutes, until tender. Drain well and let cool.
　　Transfer to a serving bowl and stir in the radishes.

2　To make the dressing, place the yogurt and milk in a bowl and
　　whisk until smooth. Stir in the gherkins and dill and season with
　　salt and pepper.

3　Pour the dressing over the potatoes and radishes and toss to coat.
　　Add the red onion and arugula leaves and mix gently. Serve.

31

PUMPKIN

Pumpkins contain the orange nutrients alpha- and beta-carotene and lutein, powerful antiaging nutrients that protect you against skin damage from sunlight.

These fat-soluble carotenoids are needed to protect fatty areas in, for example, the skin, heart, eyes, brain, and liver. As a winter vegetable, pumpkin is well placed to protect us when we need it most. We eat more fat in the winter and lay down more fat stores for insulation and to use as energy during the cold months. The seeds of pumpkin are especially nutrient-rich, while the flesh contains malic acid—also found in apples and plums—that is needed by every cell in the body for renewal and to make repairs. In combination with the protective carotenoids, it helps keep skin firm, bones strong, and our organs youthful.

- Contains phytosterols, needed for immune function and cholesterol regulation.
- Contains vitamin B_2 to activate folate, and vitamin B_6 to process fats and proteins from food to repair and rejuvenate body tissues and mucus membranes.
- Vitamin E supports fertility and young-looking skin.

Practical tips:
Like most squash, pumpkin can be boiled, steamed, baked, or roasted, and used to make both sweet and savory dishes. Pumpkin is sometimes oversweetened, especially in some traditional American dishes, which masks its delicate flavor. Experiment with less sugar if using in sweet recipes.

DID YOU KNOW?

The name pumpkin originally comes from the Greek *peponi*, meaning "large melon." The French then called it *pompon*, and the British opted for *pumpion*, before finally taking the American name.

MAJOR NUTRIENTS PER ¾ CUP CUBED PUMPKIN

Calories	13
Total fat	0.1 g
Protein	1 g
Carbohydrate	6.5 g
Fiber	0.5 g
Vitamin C	9 mg
Vitamin E	1.06 mg
Vitamin B_2	0.11 mg
Vitamin B_5	0.06 mg
Folate	16 mcg
Beta-carotene	3,100 mcg
Lutein/Zeaxanthin	1,500 mcg
Phytosterols	12 mg

Carrot and pumpkin curry

SERVES 4

²⁄₃ cup low-salt
   vegetable stock
1-inch/2.5-cm piece fresh
   galangal, sliced
2 garlic cloves, chopped
1 lemongrass stalk (white part only),
   finely chopped
2 fresh red chiles, seeded
   and chopped
4 carrots, peeled and cut
   into chunks
8 oz/225 g pumpkin, peeled,
   seeded and cut into cubes
2 tbsp peanut or coconut oil
2 shallots, finely chopped
3 tbsp Thai yellow curry paste
1¾ cups coconut milk
4–6 fresh Thai basil sprigs
2 tbsp lightly toasted pumpkin
   seeds, for garnishing

Method

1 Pour the stock into a large saucepan and bring to a boil. Add
   the galangal, half the garlic, the lemongrass, and chiles and
   simmer for 5 minutes. Add the carrots and pumpkin and simmer
   for 5–6 minutes, until tender.

2 Meanwhile, heat the oil in a wok or skillet and stir-fry the shallots
   and the remaining garlic for 2–3 minutes. Add the curry paste and
   stir-fry for 1–2 minutes.

3 Stir the shallot mixture into the saucepan and add the coconut milk
   and Thai basil. Simmer for 2–3 minutes. Serve hot, sprinkled with
   the toasted pumpkin seeds.

32

CUCUMBER

Cucumber is a squash long used for its cooling effects, inside and outside the body, reducing inflammation and speeding repair for young-looking skin.

As well as drinking fluids directly, we need to receive water from the plant foods we eat. The high water content of cucumber makes it a hydrating food that prevents dryness and wrinkling of the skin, as well as helping to remove the toxins that can age us. Cucumber is a recommended food in the DASH diet (Dietary Approaches to Stop Hypertension) as it is rich in potassium, magnesium, and fiber, so works naturally to reduce high blood pressure by balancing the fluid in the body. The vitamin C and caffeic acid in cucumbers also help rid the body of excess fluid as they both help prevent water retention.

- Source of silica, a trace mineral needed for a healthy complexion.
- Cucumber juice is known to alleviate the symptoms of rheumatic conditions and keep joints healthy and young.
- Contains the trace mineral molybdenum, which is needed to keep bones and teeth strong and healthy.

Practical tips:
Cucumber combines well with other vegetables and fruits. Include its skin in juices and salads for maximum nutrition. The juice can also be applied directly to cuts, burns, and skin conditions to bring immediate cooling relief, or you can puree the whole vegetable in a blender for use as a rejuvenating poultice or face mask, with avocado if you have some. Cucumber slices placed on the eyes will reduce puffiness and signs of tiredness.

DID YOU KNOW?

The saying "cool as a cucumber" comes from the fact that the inside of a cucumber can be 20°F/6.6°C cooler than the outside air.

MAJOR NUTRIENTS PER 1 CUP SLICED CUCUMBER

Calories	16
Total fat	0.11 g
Protein	0.65 g
Carbohydrate	3.63 g
Fiber	0.5 g
Vitamin C	2.8 mg
Vitamin B5	0.26 mg
Magnesium	13 mg
Potassium	147 mg
Silica	Trace
Molybdenum	Trace

Cucumber smoothie

SERVES 1

½ cucumber

2 apples

1 cup fresh cilantro,
    leaves and stems

Method

1 Cut a few long strips from the cucumber and set aside. Juice the apple, cilantro, and cucumber together. Pour into glasses, add the cucumber strips, and serve.

33

MAITAKE MUSHROOMS

Used extensively in Japanese and Chinese medicine for ailments affecting most body systems, maitake have been traditionally used for youth and longevity.

Research has supported anecdotal belief in the benefits of maitake for keeping the heart healthy and youthful, which they achieve by regulating blood pressure, lowering triglycerides (fats in the bloodstream), and lowering levels of "bad" LDL cholesterol. Maitake regulate fats in the body generally, including those in the liver and brain, and have a positive effect on weight loss. This is also linked to their ability to regulate glucose and insulin, thereby balancing blood-sugar levels, appetite, cravings, and energy levels. Supplements of maitake may be taken in order to benefit more fully from its therapeutic effects, but eating the mushrooms alongside other beneficial foods is sufficient to assist in weight loss.

- Good nonanimal source of vitamin D, needed for healthy bones, a positive, youthful outlook, and protection against many age-related diseases.
- Contains vitamin B_3, needed to keep the metabolism up and the body burning calories, for weight maintenance.
- Contains choline, a B vitamin that helps the liver remove aging toxins from the body.

Practical tips:
The whole maitake mushroom can be eaten. If using fresh, wash thoroughly and then use as any other mushroom. They are more readily available dried; rehydrate by soaking in lukewarm water and add to soups and stews (with the soaking liquid) or to stir-fries.

DID YOU KNOW?

Native to both Japan and North America, where they grow at the base of oak trees and can reach a weight of 44 lb/20 kg, maitake are also known as hen of the woods, ram's head, and sheep's head.

MAJOR NUTRIENTS PER 1¾ oz/50 G MAITAKE MUSHROOMS

Calories	15.5
Total fat	0.1 g
Protein	0.97 g
Carbohydrate	3.48 g
Fiber	1.4 g
Choline	25.5 mg
Vitamin D	590.5 IU
Vitamin B_3	3.3 mg

Mushroom fajitas

SERVES 4

2 tbsp olive or peanut oil

1 lb 2 oz/500 g mixed
   mushrooms (maitake,
   shiitake, and cremini), sliced

1 onion, sliced

1 red bell pepper, seeded
   and sliced

1 yellow bell pepper, seeded
   and sliced

1 garlic clove, crushed

¼–½ tsp cayenne pepper

juice and grated rind of 2 limes

1 tsp dried oregano

8 tortillas

salt and pepper

salsa and lime wedges, for serving

Method

1 Heat the oil in a large heavy-bottom skillet. Add the mushrooms, onion, red and yellow bell peppers, and garlic and stir-fry for 8–10 minutes, until the vegetables are cooked.

2 Add the cayenne pepper, lime juice and rind, and oregano. Season with salt and pepper to taste and cook for an additional 2 minutes.

3 Meanwhile, heat the tortillas according to the package directions. Divide the mushroom mixture among the warmed tortillas, roll up, and serve with the salsa and lime wedges.

34

FENNEL

The smell of fennel comes from anethole, a chemical that reduces aging inflammation and protects the liver from toxins that can lead to wrinkles and age spots.

A member of the Umbelliferae family and a cousin of parsley, carrots, dill, and coriander, fennel has a long medicinal history. It is traditionally used to ease digestive gas buildup, shed water retention by acting as a diuretic, and lower high blood pressure. Fennel is full of compounds that provide strong antioxidant activity, including two of the most potent found: rutin and quercetin. Rutin tones blood vessels to help prevent varicose veins and easy bruising, increases nourishing circulation, and is anti-inflammatory. Quercetin helps prevent heart disease, respiratory problems, and cancer, and as a natural antihistamine, alleviates allergic reactions.

- A known stimulant, quercetin supplies youthful zest without causing a subsequent energy dip.
- Potassium keeps brain and muscle nerves firing and able to react quickly.
- Vitamin C helps heal scars and create antistress hormones, encouraging a youthful appearance.

Practical tips:
Good raw, sliced in salads, and cooked by stir-frying, sautéeing, braising, stewing, roasting, or broiling. Fennel has a piquant taste that adds interest and works particularly well with fish. Prepare by chopping off the darker green stalk and slicing up the lighter bulb, cutting out the tougher part where the root meets.

DID YOU KNOW?

It is common practice in India to chew fennel seeds after a meal to help digestion and ward off the bad breath that digestive disorders can cause.

MAJOR NUTRIENTS PER HALF BULB FENNEL

Calories	12
Total fat	Trace
Protein	0.9 g
Carbohydrate	1.8 g
Fiber	2.4 g
Vitamin C	5 mg
Folate	42 mcg
Potassium	440 mg

Sea bream with fennel and tomato butter

SERVES 4

4 sea bream fillets, skin on, about
6 oz/175 g each
2 tbsp olive oil
salt and pepper
fresh parsley sprigs, for garnishing

Baked fennel
4 fennel bulbs, trimmed
juice of ½ lemon
6 tbsp olive oil

Tomato butter sauce
8 large vine-ripened tomatoes
1 tbsp extra virgin olive oil
5 tbsp butter, cut into cubes

Method

1 Preheat the oven to 400°F/200°C. For the baked fennel, slice the fennel bulbs lengthwise and put in a casserole. Sprinkle with the lemon juice. Season with salt and pepper to taste and pour over the olive oil. Cover with foil and bake in the preheated oven for 30 minutes, or until tender. Remove from the oven, uncover, and return to the oven for an additional 10 minutes.

2 Meanwhile, to make the sauce, put the tomatoes in a food processor and process to a puree. Pass through a strainer into a medium saucepan. Heat gently, then stir in the extra virgin olive oil. Set aside.

3 Brush the fish fillets with a little of the olive oil and season lightly with salt and pepper. Heat the remaining oil in an ovenproof skillet over medium–high heat, add the fish fillets, skin-side down, and cook for 1 minute. Turn the fillets over and cook for an additional minute. Transfer to the oven and cook for 2–3 minutes.

4 Just before serving, gently reheat the sauce and whisk in the butter, cube by cube, until fully incorporated. Season with salt and pepper to taste.

5 Divide the fennel among 4 warmed plates and top each portion with a fish fillet. Spoon the sauce around and serve immediately, garnished with parsley sprigs.

35

CAULIFLOWER

Cauliflower contains the same potent cleansing and rejuvenating sulfur compounds as the other members of the brassica family, such as Brussels sprouts.

One of these compounds, sulforaphane, has been found to help prevent adult-onset diabetes and destroy invading microbes, such as bacteria and viruses. It can also work as an antioxidant through enzymes produced in the liver, helping repair areas of the body that have been damaged. Research has shown this wonder substance helps prevent cancer and the progression of tumors by stopping cancer cells spreading and actively killing them off. Another sulfur compound in cauliflower, indole-3-carbinol, appears to lower estrogen, thereby helping to prevent cancers of the breast and prostate as well as regulating female hormones, keeping women youthful post menopause.

- Source of vitamin B_6, used to unlock energy from the food we eat for skin and bone renewal.
- Vitamin C helps the liver remove damaging, aging toxins.
- Vitamin C and vitamin B_5 support the adrenal glands and so help us cope with stress, an important factor in staying young.

Practical tips:
Serve raw florets with dips or use in a salad. Remove the outer leaves and steam a whole cauliflower for about 10 minutes or separate into florets and steam for about 6 minutes. While cooking, test regularly with a knife to make sure it doesn't overcook. Over-cooked cauliflower evokes memories of unpleasant school meals, but when cooked properly it is crunchy and delicious.

DID YOU KNOW?

A purple cauliflower variety, called "Purple Cape," has recently been developed so that fans of cauliflower can take on beneficial proanthocyanidins, the antioxidants also found in purple sprouting broccoli.

MAJOR NUTRIENTS PER ¾ CUP FLORETS CAULIFLOWER

Calories	25
Total fat	0 g
Protein	2 g
Carbohydrate	5 g
Fiber	2.5 g
Vitamin C	46 mg
Vitamin B_5	0.65 mg
Vitamin B_6	0.22 mg
Folate	57 mg

Garlic and chili potatoes with cauliflower

SERVES 4

12 oz/350 g new potatoes
1 small cauliflower
2 tbsp olive oil
1 tsp black or brown
   mustard seeds
1 tsp cumin seeds
5 large garlic cloves, lightly
   crushed, then chopped
1–2 fresh green chiles,
   finely chopped
   (seeded, if you like)
½ tsp ground turmeric
½ tsp salt, or to taste
2 tbsp chopped fresh
   cilantro leaves

Method

1 Cook the potatoes in their skins in a saucepan of boiling water for 20 minutes, or until tender. Drain, then soak in cold water for 30 minutes. Peel them, if you like, then halve or quarter according to their size—they should be a similar size to the cauliflower florets (see below).

2 Meanwhile, divide the cauliflower into about 1-inch/ 2.5-cm florets and blanch in a large saucepan of boiling salted water for 3 minutes.

Drain and plunge into iced water to prevent further cooking, then drain again.

3 Heat the oil in a medium saucepan over medium heat. When hot, but not smoking, add the mustard seeds, then the cumin seeds.

4 Remove from the heat and add the garlic and chiles. Return to low heat and cook, stirring, until the garlic has a light brown tinge.

5 Stir in the turmeric, followed by the cauliflower and the potatoes. Add the salt, increase the heat slightly, and cook, stirring, until the vegetables are well blended with all the spices and everything is heated through.

6 Stir in the cilantro, remove from the heat, and serve the vegetables immediately.

36

ENDIVE

The oils that give endive its bitter taste help us absorb the nutrients we need from food to repair all body parts to stay young.

Endive's bitter juices are cholegenic, meaning that they cause bile to be produced in the liver, which regulates cholesterol and helps break down the fats that we eat. They also stimulate other digestive juices and act as a light laxative, keeping bowel function regular, and ensuring that damaging and aging toxins are eliminated from the body. Endive acts as a diuretic, cleaning out the kidneys as it increases urination and helps the body shed excess fluid that can collect as bloating or puffiness around the eyes, ankles, fingers, thighs, and abdomen.

- Contains the amino acids tyrosine and phenylalanine that help regulate appetite and curb cravings to keep weight down.
- Tyrosine also produces hormones that are vital for energy and coping with the effects of stress, which can be very aging.
- Contains vitamin K, which is good for youthful bones and a healthy heart.
- Folate and beta-carotene content keeps skin looking young and healthy.

Practical tips:
Endive is one of the chicory family, along with common chicory and radicchio. All of these have the similar bitter taste that will liven up a salad and give some kick to a soup. Many people are out of the habit of eating bitter foods, such as endive, as well as watercress and grapefruit, but they are an important part of our diet and a taste for them can be built up.

DID YOU KNOW?
Mediterranean in origin, endive was first grown nearly 5,000 years ago and eaten by the Egyptians, Greeks, and Romans, both for its taste and for its medicinal properties.

MAJOR NUTRIENTS PER 1 CUP CHOPPED ENDIVE

Calories	8.5
Total fat	0.1 g
Protein	0.63 g
Carbohydrate	1.68 g
Fiber	1.5 g
Vitamin C	3.3 mg
Vitamin K	115.5 mg
Folate	71 mg
Beta-carotene	650 mcg
Tyrosine	0.02 mg
Phenylalanine	0.03 mg

Endive salad with peaches and walnuts

SERVES 4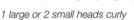

1 large or 2 small heads curly
   endive
2 ripe peaches
½ cup walnut pieces
1 tbsp chopped chives
2 tbsp dried cranberries

French dressing

3 tbsp extra virgin olive oil
1 tbsp white wine vinegar
¼ tsp good-quality honey
¼ tsp Dijon mustard
salt and pepper

Method

1 Separate the endive leaves gently and halve any larger ones.
    Arrange in a serving bowl or on individual plates.
2 To make the dressing, combine the oil, vinegar, honey, mustard,
    and seasoning in a small bowl.
3 Just before you are ready to serve, peel, pit, and cut each
    peach into slim wedges and arrange over the endive. Drizzle
    the dressing over the salad. Scatter the walnut pieces, chives,
    and cranberries over the salad to serve.

37

SWISS CHARD

Swiss chard is similar to spinach and beets, sharing the same bitter and slightly salty taste that helps regulate appetite and keep weight at a healthy level.

The dark color of Swiss chard leaves testifies to an abundance of the protective antioxidant chemical proanthocyanidins, which is excellent for circulation and heart health, and helps to protect against varicose veins. The folate and vitamin C in Swiss chard promote the regrowth of tissues and veins and prevent premature aging. The leaves also contain calcium and magnesium, which work together to promote heart and bone health. These are known as the "calming minerals" because they soothe the nervous system and help prevent the anxiety, depression, high blood pressure, and insomnia that stress may cause.

- Vitamin C and magnesium help prevent heart disease and keep the heart young so it can pump replenishing nutrients around the body.
- Vitamin K helps slow the action of osteoclasts, cells that break down bone, and activates osteocalcin, which anchors calcium into bone to help regrowth, keeping your skeleton young.
- Cleansing properties help promote smooth skin and prevent the build up of cellulite.

Practical tips:
When young, Swiss chard leaves can be eaten raw in salads, whereas the more bitter taste of the older leaves should be broken down through cooking. Swiss chard is most popularly eaten sautéed. Keep in the refrigerator in a plastic bag, or blanch and then freeze.

DID YOU KNOW?

Swiss chard is not native to Switzerland but was named by the Swiss botanist Koch. It is one of the most nutritious leafy vegetables you can eat, and is associated with good mental health and memory.

MAJOR NUTRIENTS PER 2¾ CUPS CHOPPED SWISS CHARD

Calories	19
Total fat	0.2 g
Protein	1.8 g
Carbohydrate	3.74 g
Fiber	1.6 g
Vitamin C	30 mg
Vitamin K	830 mcg
Folate	14 mcg
Calcium	51 mg
Magnesium	81 mg

Monkfish in Swiss chard parcels

SERVES 4　　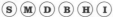

1 lb 2 oz/500 g Swiss chard,
　trimmed
1 lb 4 oz/550 g monkfish fillet,
　cut into bite-size pieces
1½ tbsp lime juice
⅔ cup live Greek-style yogurt
2 egg yolks, lightly beaten
pinch of paprika
3 tbsp butter
½ cup white wine
salt and pepper

Method

1　Cut the stems from the Swiss chard leaves and set aside. Steam 8 leaves for 15 seconds, then remove and spread out on a counter. Shred any remaining leaves.

2　Mix together the pieces of fish, lime juice, and 5 tablespoons of the yogurt in a bowl. Stir in the egg yolks, add the paprika, and season to taste.

3　Divide the fish mixture equally among the steamed leaves, then roll up, tucking in the sides. Secure with toothpicks or tie with kitchen string.

4　Bring a saucepan of water to a boil and line a steamer with wax paper. Put the rolls in the steamer in a single layer, cover with a tight-fitting lid, and steam for 15–20 minutes, until tender.

5　Meanwhile, finely chop the reserved Swiss chard stems. Melt the butter in a skillet, add the stems, and cook over low heat, stirring occasionally, for 10 minutes, until tender. Stir in the white wine and bring to a boil.

6　Transfer the Swiss chard stem mixture to a blender or food processor, add the remaining yogurt, and process until smooth. Scrape the mixture into a saucepan, add the shredded Swiss chard leaves, and cook over low heat, stirring constantly, until thickened. Season to taste.

7　Remove the fish parcels from the steamer. Remove and discard the toothpicks or kitchen string and transfer to a serving dish. Spoon the sauce into the dish and serve immediately.

38 POTATOES

Potatoes are rich in minerals that you need for the effective functioning of your brain and muscles, to keep you thinking and moving youthfully.

The high starchy carbohydrate content of potatoes makes them number one on the Satiety Index, which scores foods according to how much they satisfy our hunger right after eating them. Healthy boiled potatoes are actually three times as satisfying as fried potatoes and can be very helpful in curbing cravings for sweet, unhealthy foods that lead to aging weight gain. Potatoes also provide dense fuel for people under stress or for exercising and can help regulate energy and weight.

- Source of kukoamines, also found in goji berries, which along with the high potassium content help lower blood pressure.
- Contains vitamin B_6 needed to produce the neurotransmitter GABA that helps us cope with stress, a major factor in staying young.
- Vitamin C protects sensitive brain and nerve cells from toxins, helping to keep our brains sharp and our muscles responsive.

Practical tips:
Most nutrients in potatoes are found just under the skins, and removing these also cuts out the rich fiber there. The older and larger potatoes have a higher score on the Glycemic Index (GI), meaning that their sugars hit the bloodstream quicker, upsetting blood sugar balance. New potatoes with their skins intact are the healthiest option.

DID YOU KNOW?

Potatoes are the most grown and eaten vegetable in the world, but their high starch content excludes them from our "five a day" fruit and vegetable count.

MAJOR NUTRIENTS PER ⅔ CUP DICED POTATOES

Calories	77
Total fat	0.1 g
Protein	2 g
Carbohydrate	19 g
Fiber	2.2 g
Vitamin C	20 mg
Vitamin B_6	0.25 mg
Potassium	421 mg

Warm new potato and lentil salad

SERVES 6

scant ½ cup French green lentils
1 lb/450 g new potatoes
6 scallions
1 tbsp extra virgin olive oil
2 tbsp balsamic vinegar
salt and pepper

Method

1 Bring a large pan of water to a boil.
2 Rinse the lentils, then cook for about 20 minutes, or until tender. Drain, rinse, and set aside.
3 Meanwhile, steam or boil the potatoes until they are soft all the way through. Drain and halve.
4 Trim the base from the scallions and cut into slices.
5 Put the lentils, potatoes, and scallions into a serving dish and toss with the olive oil and vinegar. Season with plenty of pepper and a little salt if required.

39 BOK CHOY

This is a cruciferous vegetable in the same family as cabbage, broccoli, kale, and Brussels sprouts, and offers the same protective, rejuvenating properties.

The anticancer properties of cruciferous vegetables are well documented. Research in Singapore found that these vegetables, including bok choy, reduce the risk of lung cancer in nonsmokers by 30 percent and in smokers by an astonishing 69 percent. Bok choy also enhances and balances all aspects of liver detoxification, a remedy against the ravaging effects of stress, pollution, and the aging factors in our modern environment. Bok choy contains a higher amount of vitamin A than other cabbages and so particularly protects the liver from aging damage from sugar, alcohol, and medications as it is stored in high amounts in this organ.

• High calcium content keeps bones, teeth, and joints healthy and prevents osteoporosis; it also supports heart health and optimum brain function.
• Contains beta-carotene that can be converted to vitamin A and used to fight toxins that cause premature aging.
• Vitamin C enables all other antioxidants to work effectively and so protect and repair the skin, bones, brain, and heart to keep you looking and feeling young.

Practical tips:
Typically used in stir-fries and soups, such as miso, bok choy is quicker to cook and lighter than other cabbage, and tastes particularly good when it retains its crunchiness. Darker varieties may need longer to cook than the smaller, light ones.

DID YOU KNOW?

Bok choy literally means "white vegetable" in Chinese and is also spelled pak choi. The variety used today is similar to one cultivated in the 14th century.

MAJOR NUTRIENTS PER 1½ CUPS SHREDDED BOK CHOY

Calories	13
Total fat	0.2 g
Protein	1.5 g
Carbohydrate	2.2 g
Fiber	1 g
Vitamin C	45 mg
Vitamin A	4,468 IU
Folate	66 mcg
Beta-carotene	2,681 mcg
Calcium	105 mg
Magnesium	19 mg

Stir-fried bok choy

SERVES 6

2 tbsp olive oil

2 large garlic cloves, thinly sliced

1½–2 lb/675–900 g bok choy,

   leaves separated

Thai fish sauce, to taste

pepper

Method

1 Heat the oil in a wok or large skillet over high heat, then add the garlic and stir-fry for 3 minutes, or until golden.

2 Add the bok choy and stir-fry for 2–4 minutes, or until wilted and tender. Season with fish sauce and pepper to taste.

40

ROMAINE LETTUCE

Romaine or cos lettuce is regarded as a type of dark green leafy vegetable. Its foliage contains all the power of folate necessary to regenerate baby-fresh skin.

The darker the leaf, the more folate it contains and the better it is for skin renewal and regeneration. Folate is required for all growth in the body as it forms the genetic material DNA, necessary to build all cells. Our cells are continually being renewed and replaced throughout life, but this process can decline with age. Folate is especially important during pregnancy, and may also help prevent cervical cancer, heart problems, and osteoporosis. It promotes restful sleep and good mood by releasing the neurotransmitter serotonin, which also helps regulate appetite and sugar cravings and prevent the overeating that can lead to weight gain.

- Contains the antioxidant carotenoids that protect skin from UV damage, such as wrinkles, and the dark spots caused by heat oxidation.
- The fiber present eliminates toxins that can stop the process of cell regeneration and age the body prematurely.
- The bitter taste stimulates our digestive juices when it hits the tongue, improving digestion of the meal as a whole, not only the leaves.

Practical tips:
Romaine or cos lettuce is usually eaten in a salad, but with its thick stalk is sturdy enough to withstand heat and, therefore, may be cooked lightly in stir-fries. It is the lettuce usually used in Caesar salad and Middle Eastern cuisine.

DID YOU KNOW?

The thick ribs on the outer leaves contain a milky fluid that explains the lettuce's characteristic bitter-sharp taste, reminiscent of a herb.

MAJOR NUTRIENTS PER 2 CUPS SHREDDED ROMAINE LETTUCE

Calories	17
Total fat	0.3 g
Protein	1.2 g
Carbohydrate	3.3 g
Fiber	2.1 g
Vitamin C	24 mg
Folate	136 mcg
Calcium	33 mg
Potassium	247 mg

Braised lettuce and peas

SERVES 4

1 tbsp butter or olive oil

1 small onion, finely chopped

2 Romaine lettuce

3½ cups small fresh or frozen peas

heaping ¾ cup fresh chicken or
   low-salt vegetable stock

4 tbsp plain live yogurt

salt and pepper

Method

1 Melt the butter or heat the oil in a large sauté pan with a lid. Fry the onion gently over medium heat for about 5 minutes, until softened.

2 Remove any damaged or tough outer leaves from the lettuce and trim the bases. Cut in half lengthwise and arrange, cut-side up, on top of the onions. Scatter the peas around evenly.

3 Season and pour over the stock. Put the lid on, reduce the heat to very low, and simmer for 10 minutes.

4 Stir in the yogurt and simmer the vegetables for 1 minute to heat through before serving.

41

GREEN BEANS

Green beans, peas, and beans are all legumes, with a high protein content that is essential for the revitalization of the skin, bones, and muscles.

Plant protein is an important part of any diet, whether you eat animal products or not. We need protein for all structures in the body to do the continual work of rebuilding skin, bone, teeth, hair, and nails. The effects of too little protein are a dull complexion, lank hair, and brittle nails. Whereas animal protein is acid-forming in the body, protein derived from plants, such as beans, is more alkaline, the optimal state when it comes to detoxification, repair, and regulation of the metabolism. Plant sources also come with good levels of fiber that help clear harmful waste from the body, promote good digestion, and full absorption of the wide range of nutrients we need to stay young.

- Vitamin B_6 and folate reduce homocysteine levels in the blood, a substance that can create the risk of heart disease.
- The B vitamins unlock energy from all the food we eat so that it can be used as fuel for all cell repair. Deficiency symptoms include dull skin and hair, poor nail health, cracked lips and spots, as well as fatigue, anxiety, insomnia, and depression.
- Contains choline, which helps move fatty deposits out of the liver and protects us from the harmful and aging effects of alcohol.

Practical tips:
Buy beans loose from a market where possible so that you can select those with a smooth feel, bright green color, and a pleasing snap when broken in half. They are a key ingredient in Salad Niçoise.

DID YOU KNOW?

Green beans are the unripe fruit of any bean plant. They are also referred to as snap beans and string beans. French beans are a type of green bean with thinner, larger pods.

MAJOR NUTRIENTS PER 1 CUP 1-INCH/2.5-CM PIECES GREEN BEANS

Calories	31
Total fat	0.1 g
Protein	1.8 g
Carbohydrate	7.1 g
Fiber	3.6 g
Vitamin C	16 mg
Vitamin B_2	0.6 mg
Vitamin B_3	0.8 mg
Vitamin B_5	21 mcg
Vitamin B_6	151 mg
Folate	25 mg
Choline	0.7 mg

Green beans with almonds and lemon

SERVES 4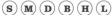

1 lb 2 oz/500 g green beans,
  trimmed
1 lemon
3 tbsp olive oil
heaping ½ cup slivered almonds
1 tsp ground sweet paprika
salt

Method

1 Bring a saucepan of lightly salted water to a boil and cook the beans for 3–4 minutes, or until just tender but still with some bite. Refresh under cold running water and then dry thoroughly in a clean dish towel or paper towels.

2 Remove 2 teaspoons of the lemon rind with a fine parer, being careful not to remove the pith. Juice the lemon.

3 Heat a little of the oil in a large skillet and add the slivered almonds. Stir over medium–high heat until they begin to turn golden brown. Immediately take the skillet off the heat, as they will burn quickly once past this stage if left over high heat.

4 Stir in the beans, the remaining oil, the lemon rind, juice, and sweet paprika, with a pinch of salt, if liked. Return the skillet to a medium heat and stir for 1–2 minutes until the beans are heated through, then serve.

MEAT, FISH, DAIRY, AND EGGS

These foods form the protein basis of a well-rounded day's diet, keeping your bones and muscles continually renewed. A varied spread of protein foods also provides the healthy fats that you need to retain a youthful heart and brain.

(S) Skin, hair, and nails

(M) Mobility and strength

(D) Digestive/detoxification health

(B) Brain health

(H) Heart health

(I) Immunity-supporting antioxidant

42

LAMB

Lamb is an energy-rich, high-quality meat that contains important nutrients for immunity and the slowing down of aging.

Animal, as well as plant sources of food, supply antioxidants that support immunity. Lamb is rich in the antioxidant trace minerals zinc and selenium. These produce liver enzymes that are our most powerful defense against free radicals, the harmful molecules that damage and age all parts of the body, from the skin to the internal organs. Another antioxidant that is present in lamb, coenzyme Q-10, works to protect the heart and to provide energy for the body as a whole. Coenzyme Q-10 has also been shown to reduce incidences of congestive heart failure, Alzheimer's disease, Parkinson's disease, chronic fatigue, breast cancer, and gum disease.

- Quality source of protein, for repairing and rebuilding worn-out cells. A single serving provides around 60 percent of your daily requirements.
- Contains the B vitamins that support vitality in every cell of the body to keep you looking and feeling young.
- Although high in saturated fat, it also contains beneficial levels of heart-healthy monounsaturated fats.

Practical tips:
As a red meat, lamb is generally higher in saturated fat than white. You don't need to eat it often to enjoy its benefits. It's best to be picky about the cuts you choose—chops are the healthiest option. Lamb also makes a delicious burger alternative to beef, and works well with apricots and prunes, as in Middle Eastern tagines.

DID YOU KNOW?

Lamb is the meat of a sheep that is under a year old. After a year, the sheep and its meat are known as yearling. Beyond two years, when the sheep develops two permanent incisor teeth, it is classed as mutton.

MAJOR NUTRIENTS PER 3½ oz/100 g LAMB

Calories	229
Total fat	16.97 g
Saturated fat	8.18 g
Monounsaturated fat	62.5 g
Protein	5.1 g
Carbohydrate	3.5 mg
Fiber	628 mg
Vitamin B₂	92 mg
Vitamin B₃	74 mg
Vitamin B₅	0.56 mg
Vitamin B₆	0.34 mg
Vitamin B₁₂	2.47 mg
Iron	1.43 mg
Zinc	3.67 mg
Selenium	7.5 mg

Broiled lamb with yogurt and herb dressing

SERVES 4

2 tbsp olive oil,
  plus extra for broiling
1 tbsp tomato paste
½ tbsp ground cumin
1 tsp lemon juice
1 garlic clove, crushed
pinch of cayenne pepper
1 lb 2 oz/500 g lamb shoulder,
  trimmed, with excess fat
  removed, and sliced
salt and pepper
lightly toasted sesame seeds
  and fresh parsley sprig,
  for garnishing

Dressing

2 tbsp fresh lemon juice
1 tsp good-quality honey
⅓ cup live Greek-style yogurt
2 tbsp finely shredded fresh mint
2 tbsp chopped fresh parsley
1 tbsp finely snipped fresh chives
salt and pepper

Method

1 Mix the 2 tablespoons oil, tomato paste, cumin, lemon juice, garlic, cayenne, and salt and pepper to taste, together in a nonmetallic bowl. Add the lamb slices and rub all over with the marinade. Cover the bowl and marinate the lamb in the refrigerator for at least 2 hours, but ideally overnight.

2 Meanwhile, to make the dressing, whisk the lemon juice and honey together until the honey dissolves. Whisk in the yogurt until well blended. Stir in the herbs and add salt and pepper to taste. Cover and chill until required.

3 Remove the lamb from the refrigerator 15 minutes before you are ready to cook. Heat the broiler to its highest setting and lightly brush the broil rack with oil. Broil the lamb, turning once, for 10 minutes for medium and 12 minutes for well done. Let the lamb cool completely, then cover and chill until required.

4 Thinly slice the lamb, then divide among 4 plates. Adjust the seasoning in the dressing, if necessary, then spoon over the lamb slices. To serve, sprinkle with toasted sesame seeds and garnish with the parsley sprig.

43

FREE-RANGE CHICKEN

The inclusion of dense protein found in free-range chicken in the diet helps prevent the body from aging prematurely as a result of stress.

The human body consists of 22 percent protein, and just under half of this is muscle. Your muscles need continual replenishment, especially after exercise, in order for the body to maintain youthful mobility and posture. Stress uses up protein in the body to make adrenaline, but chicken in the diet can replace it in a way that the body finds easy to absorb. Chicken that has been reared healthily can also provide the B vitamins needed to maintain energy levels and good brain function.

• Protein makes the collagen that is needed on a daily basis to rejuvenate skin, hair, nails, and the internal organs.
• Contains hyaluronic acid, which holds water in collagen in order to keep the body hydrated and the skin firm.
• Contains glutamic acid, the main protein in human muscle, which ensures strength and rapid response.
• The antioxidant mineral selenium helps combat toxic metals that contribute to aging, such as mercury, lead, and aluminum.

Practical tips:
Choose your chicken wisely. Battery-farmed birds will not have used their muscles sufficiently to develop as a source of protein. They can also be much higher in harmful fats than free-range birds. Although it is a more expensive option, organic chicken is better quality and you can eat it less frequently to balance out the cost.

DID YOU KNOW?
Chicken is the world's primary animal protein source, with just 3½ oz/100 g providing two-thirds of what we need daily to replenish skin, bone, and muscle.

MAJOR NUTRIENTS PER 3½ OZ/100 G CHICKEN, SKIN REMOVED

Calories	114
Total fat	2.59 g
Saturated fat	0.57 g
Monounsaturated fat	0.76 g
Protein	21.23 g
Carbohydrate	0 mg
Fiber	0 mg
Vitamin B$_3$	10.43 mg
Vitamin B$_5$	1.43 mcg
Vitamin B$_6$	0.75 mg
Selenium	32 mcg
Glutamic acid	3.15 g

Thai-spiced chicken with zucchini

SERVES 4

1 tbsp olive oil

1 garlic clove, finely chopped

1-inch/2.5-cm piece fresh ginger,
    peeled and finely chopped

1 small fresh red chile, seeded and
    finely chopped

12 oz/350 g skinless, boneless
    free-range chicken breasts,
    cut into thin strips

1 tbsp Thai seven-spice seasoning

1 red bell pepper and 1 yellow bell
    pepper, seeded and sliced

2 zucchini, thinly sliced

8 oz/227 g canned bamboo
    shoots, drained

2 tbsp apple juice

1 tbsp light soy sauce

2 tbsp chopped fresh cilantro,
    plus extra for garnishing

salt and pepper

Method

1 Heat the olive oil in a nonstick wok or large skillet. Add the chopped garlic, ginger, and chile, and stir-fry for 30 seconds to release the flavors.

2 Add the chicken and Thai seasoning and stir-fry for about 4 minutes, or until the chicken has colored all over. Add the bell peppers and zucchini and stir-fry for 1–2 minutes, or until slightly softened.

3 Stir in the bamboo shoots and stir-fry for an additional 2–3 minutes, or until the chicken is cooked through and tender. Add the apple juice, soy sauce, and seasoning and sizzle for 1–2 minutes.

4 Stir in the chopped cilantro and serve immediately, garnished with extra cilantro.

44 VENISON

Venison has recently grown in popularity. It is similar to beef but is leaner, providing dense protein without the heart-clogging saturated fat content.

This protein combines with a great B-vitamin profile to keep the body intact and youthful. It includes the sulfur amino acids taurine and cystine, which fight hard to keep aging at bay by ridding the body of unwanted hormones, medications, and alcohol. If these are allowed to keep circulating, the body becomes tired, ill, and unable to heal and renew. Taurine and cystine also help hold essential minerals in the body, tonify the blood, prevent heart disease, and improve circulation to keep skin healthy and glowing.

- Vitamins B_{12} and B_6 clear the brain and heart of the damaging substance homocysteine, which can lead to dementia and heart disease.
- Vitamin B_3 keeps joints mobile and prevents osteoarthritis.
- Contains zinc, which revitalizes the skin and keeps pores clear.
- Zinc and selenium in combination create detoxification enzymes that rejuvenate cells all over the body.
- Iron moves oxygen around the body for efficient healing.

Practical tips:
Ask your butcher to let you know when venison is in season. If you buy at this time, from animals that have been hunted, you'll benefit from an absence of aging additives. Venison should be frozen for a minimum of 2 hours before use to kill off any parasites or tapeworms. Broil venison steaks and cook less tender cuts in a hearty winter stew with root vegetables and spices.

DID YOU KNOW?

Venison is game, which means it is eaten but not domesticated. Game is the most healthy form of meat to eat as it is closest to that which our ancestors would have eaten.

MAJOR NUTRIENTS PER 3½ oz/100 g VENISON

Calories	157
Total fat	7.13 g
Saturated fat	3.36 g
Monounsaturated fat	1.34 g
Protein	21.78 g
Carbohydrate	0 mg
Fiber	0 mg
Vitamin B_2	0.55 mg
Vitamin B_3	0.69 mg
Vitamin B_5	0.75 mg
Vitamin B_6	32 mcg
Vitamin B_{12}	3.15 g
Iron	2.92 g
Zinc	4.2 mg
Selenium	10 mg

Charbroiled venison steaks

SERVES 4

4 venison steaks

fresh thyme sprigs, for garnishing

Marinade

⅔ cup red wine

2 tbsp olive oil

1 tbsp red wine vinegar

1 onion, chopped

1 tbsp chopped fresh parsley

1 tbsp chopped fresh thyme

1 bay leaf

1 tsp good-quality honey

½ tsp mild mustard

salt and pepper

Method

1 Place the venison steaks in a shallow, nonmetallic dish.

2 To make the marinade, combine the wine, oil, wine vinegar, onion, fresh parsley, thyme, bay leaf, honey, and mustard, and salt and pepper to taste in a screw-top jar. Shake vigorously until well combined. Alternatively, using a fork, whisk the ingredients together in a bowl.

3 Pour the marinade mixture over the venison, cover, and let marinate in the refrigerator overnight. Turn the steaks over in the mixture occasionally so that the meat is well coated.

4 Preheat the broiler to high. Cook the venison under the hot broiler for 2 minutes on each side to seal the meat.

5 Turn down the broiler to medium and cook for an additional 4–10 minutes on each side, according to taste. Test the meat by inserting the tip of a knife into the meat—the juices will range from red when the meat is still rare to clear as the meat becomes well cooked.

6 Transfer the steaks to serving plates, garnish with fresh thyme sprigs, and serve.

45 TURKEY

A low-fat protein source, turkey helps promote a positive outlook as well as high levels of energy and vitality.

Turkey is known for its high tryptophan content, a protein constituent from which the body makes the mood, sleep, and appetite-regulating brain chemical serotonin. This is believed to be one of the reasons that we fall asleep after a heavy Thanksgiving meal; the serotonin encourages us to rest, which is a crucial component of staying young. Turkey's high protein content also helps control appetite by balancing blood-sugar levels, which curbs sugar cravings and energy fluctuations. The white meat of turkey is considered healthier than the brown meat due to its lower fat content, but the difference is small. In fact, the brown meat can actually help raise your metabolism more, making you more efficient at burning fuel, more likely to lose weight, and less susceptible to overeating.

- Iron supports energy levels by producing the cells that your body uses for fuel and helping muscles store rejuvenating oxygen.
- Glutamic acid helps balance blood sugar and combat the aging effects of stress.
- Contains the zinc that is needed to make serotonin, which makes you feel good. It is also vital in the process of repair to the body and helps you maintain a youthful appearance.

Practical tips:
Turkey can be a lower fat alternative to chicken, with many similar health benefits. A free-range bird, which has had a healthy diet itself and lived more naturally, will be leaner, taste better, and lose less water when cooked. Cook by roasting.

DID YOU KNOW?

The Aztecs domesticated the turkey and used its feathers decoratively. It was associated with Tezcatlipoca, their god of tricks.

MAJOR NUTRIENTS PER 3½ OZ/100 G TURKEY, SKIN REMOVED

Calories	111
Total fat	0.65 g
Saturated fat	0.21 g
Monounsaturated fat	0.11 g
Protein	24.6 g
Carbohydrate	0 mg
Fiber	0 mg
Vitamin B₃	6.23 mg
Vitamin B₅	0.72 mg
Vitamin B₆	0.58 mg
Iron	1.17 mg
Zinc	1.24 mg
Glutamic acid	4.02 g

Turkey salad pita

MAKES 1

small handful of baby leaf spinach, rinsed, patted dry, and shredded

½ red bell pepper, seeded and thinly sliced

½ carrot, peeled and coarsely grated

4 tbsp hummus

3 oz/85 g sliced, skinless, cooked turkey

½ tbsp sunflower seeds

1 whole wheat pita bread

salt and pepper

Method

1 Preheat the broiler to high.

2 Put the spinach leaves, red bell pepper, carrot, and hummus into a large bowl and stir together, so all the salad ingredients are coated with the hummus. Stir in the turkey and sunflower seeds and season with salt and pepper to taste.

3 Put the pita bread under the broiler for about 1 minute on each side to warm through, but do not brown. Cut it in half to make 2 "pockets" of bread.

4 Divide the salad among the bread pockets and serve.

46 PHEASANT

Pheasant is a lower-fat alternative to more common meats, and it is packed with replenishing proteins to rejuvenate the skin and bones, and to keep joints flexible.

MAJOR NUTRIENTS PER 3½ OZ/100 G PHEASANT

Calories	133
Total fat	3.25 g
Saturated fat	1.1 g
Monounsaturated fat	1.04 g
Protein	24.37 g
Carbohydrate	0 mg
Fiber	0 mg
Vitamin B$_3$	8.55 mg
Vitamin B$_5$	0.96 mg
Vitamin B$_6$	0.74 mg
Vitamin B$_{12}$	0.84 mg
Selenium	16.7 mg
Phosphorus	200 mg
Lysine	2.23 g
Leucine	2.06 g
Isoleucine	1.37 g
Valine	1.35 g

Pheasant boasts particularly good levels of the amino acids that make up the proteins we eat. These include lysine, which is known for its potent antiviral effect, and which when combined with vitamin C enhances collagen production to optimize firm skin, muscle recovery, and bone strength. In combination with the arginine that is contained in pheasant, lysine also stimulates the metabolism, boosting energy, vitality, and weight loss, and creating more proteins wherever the body needs replenishment. Leucine, isoleucine, and valine are called the Branched Chain amino acids. They make up a third of all the body's skeletal muscle, which is what keeps us mobile, upright, and moving youthfully.

• Contains phosphorus, which works with calcium for bone renewal, preventing degeneration.
• Selenium activates the thyroid hormones that promote youthful energy levels and weight regulation.
• Low calorie and high protein content boosts metabolism and helps the body stay light and spritely.

Practical tips:
Pheasants need to be hung for 1–4 weeks before eating. Like most game, a pheasant is ready at the point that the putrefaction process starts, when it has cultivated its distinctive flavor. One bird serves between two and four people. A young bird can be roasted, but an older one will need to be slow-cooked in a casserole.

Roast pheasant with red wine and herbs

SERVES 4   (S) (M) (H)

*scant ½ cup (1 stick) butter, slightly
   softened*

1 tbsp chopped fresh thyme

1 tbsp chopped fresh parsley

2 oven-ready young pheasants

4 tbsp olive oil

½ cup red wine

salt and pepper

Method

1 Preheat the oven to 375°F/190°C.

2 Put the butter in a small bowl and mix in the chopped herbs. Lift
   the skins away from the pheasant breasts, being careful not to
   tear them, and push the herb butter under the skins. Season
   with salt and pepper to taste. Pour the oil into a roasting pan,
   add the pheasants, and cook in the oven for 45 minutes,
   basting occasionally.

3 Remove from the oven, pour over the wine, then return to the oven
   and cook for an additional 15 minutes, or until cooked through.
   Check that each bird is cooked by inserting a knife between the
   legs and body. If the juices run clear, they are cooked.

4 Remove the pheasants from the oven, cover with foil, and let stand
   for 15 minutes before serving.

47 FREE-RANGE BEEF

Grass-fed, free-range beef provides fats that help with weight loss and promote youthful skin, bones, and heart.

Grass-fed cattle generally get more exercise, making their meat leaner. For every 3 oz/85 g serving, there is around 1/8 oz/6 g less fat in grass-fed beef than in its grain-fed counterpart. This is good news for calorie counters, but, more importantly, the quality of fat contained in grass-fed beef is better. Grass-fed beef contains high levels of omega-3 fatty acids, which keep the heart, joints, brain, and skin appearing youthful. Another fat, CLA (conjugated linolenic acid), comes direct from the grass, and enables stored fat to be burned as energy, which raises the metabolism and helps maintain a trim figure. Low levels of CLA in our diet have been partly linked to the rise of obesity.

- Contains four times more vitamin E than grain-fed beef, which holds back the wrinkles and prevents age spots.
- Good selenium levels lessen anxiety, depression, and fatigue. Low levels are associated with heart and bone degeneration.
- Contains the highest level of zinc in any meat, promoting clear skin and strong nails.
- Coenzyme Q-10 increases energy in all cells, especially the heart, so supports overall vigor.

Practical tips:

Ask your butcher for the best source or find a farm shop attached to its own pasture. Top round, tenderloin, and flank steak are the healthiest, leanest cuts. This is a very nutrient dense food, so you only need to eat it 2–4 times a month to get the benefits.

DID YOU KNOW?

Cattle naturally roam and feed on pasture. Cows were only fed grain when humans moved on from their role as hunter-gatherers to become farmers, around 10,000 BC.

MAJOR NUTRIENTS PER 3½ OZ/100 G BEEF

Calories	192
Total fat	12.73 g
Saturated fat	5.34 g
Monounsaturated fat	4.8 g
Protein	19.42 g
Fiber	0 mg
Vitamin B$_3$	4.82 mg
Vitamin B$_5$	0.58 mg
Vitamin B$_6$	0.36 mg
Vitamin B$_{12}$	1.97 mg
Vitamin E	930 mcg
Iron	1.99 mg
Zinc	4.55 mg
Selenium	14.2 mcg

Beef stir-fry

SERVES 4

1 tsp olive oil

5 oz/140 g grass-fed, free-range beef steak, such as top round (fat removed), cut into thin strips

1 orange bell pepper, seeded and cut into thin strips

4 scallions, trimmed and chopped

1–2 fresh jalapeño chiles, seeded and chopped

2–3 garlic cloves, chopped

1½ cups trimmed and diagonally halved snow peas

4 oz/115 g large portobello mushrooms, sliced

1 tsp hoisin sauce, or to taste

1 tbsp fresh orange juice

3 oz/85 g arugula or watercress

Method

1 Heat a wok, then add the oil and heat for 30 seconds. Add the beef and stir-fry for 1 minute, or until browned. Using a slotted spoon, remove and set aside.

2 Add the bell pepper, scallions, chiles, and garlic and stir-fry for 2 minutes. Add the snow peas and mushrooms and stir-fry for an additional 2 minutes.

3 Return the beef to the wok and add the hoisin sauce and orange juice. Stir-fry for 2–3 minutes, or until the beef is tender and the vegetables are tender but still firm to the bite. Stir in the arugula and stir-fry until it starts to wilt. Serve immediately, divided equally among 4 warmed bowls.

48 MACKEREL

Mackerel contains a good range of potent nutrients that keep skin supple, the brain sharp, and bones and joints nimble and strong.

We all need to include omega-3 fatty acids in the diet, alongside the omega-6 fatty acids found in nuts, seeds, and grains. Eating direct sources of omega 3, such as mackerel and other oily fish, is the easiest way for the body to get what it needs. One of the omega-3 fatty acids, EPA (eicosapentaenoic acid), makes a substance called resolvin that is a potent anti-inflammatory. Too little of this or too much omega 6 can make it difficult for the body to prevent aging skin inflammations, whereas getting the balance right ensures the skin is kept lubricated and plumped.

- Omega-3 fatty acids have been shown to prevent the eye damage that can occur as you get older.
- A good protein source, ensuring continued repairs to skin, bone, and other tissues.
- High vitamin B_3 content helps keep the brain lively and prevent Alzheimer's disease.
- Vitamins A and D move calcium into bones to keep them young and strong.

Practical tips:
Smoked mackerel is a handy, healthy convenience food. Fresh mackerel is even better, however, as modern smoking processes tend to involve chemicals. Bake or broil fresh when possible, or try to source fish that has been smoked traditionally.

DID YOU KNOW?

Oily fish, such as mackerel, are so-called because they can contain up to 30 percent oil. The oil acts as insulation in the cold waters they usually inhabit.

MAJOR NUTRIENTS PER 100 G/3½ OZ FRESH MACKEREL

Calories	105
Total fat	2 g
EPA	0.136 g
DHA	0.18 g
Protein	20.28 g
Fiber	0 mg
Vitamin B_3	8.6 mg
Vitamin A	727 IU
Vitamin D	9 mcg

Smoked mackerel pâté with melba toast

SERVES 4

9 oz/250 g smoked mackerel
fillets, skinned, any small bones
removed, and flaked

4½ oz/125 g drained silken tofu

2 tbsp fresh lemon juice

1 tsp grated horseradish (optional)

1 tbsp chopped fresh dill or
snipped fresh chives, plus extra
to garnish

4 slices whole wheat or rye bread

pepper

Method

1 Put the mackerel, tofu, lemon juice, and horseradish, if using, in a blender or food processor and process until smooth. Add pepper to taste. You will not need salt, as the mackerel is salty enough.

2 Stir in the fresh herbs, then transfer to a bowl, cover, and chill until about 10 minutes before serving. Sprinkle over some fresh herbs.

3 Meanwhile, preheat the broiler to high. Toast the bread on both sides until just golden brown. Using a long, serrated knife, cut off the crusts, then thinly slice each piece of toast horizontally through the center. Cut each piece into 2 triangles, then toast the untoasted sides until they are golden and the edges have curled up. Serve with the pâté.

49 ANCHOVIES

Anchovies are a delicious way to combine the benefits of omega-3 fatty acids with a healthy dose of rejuvenating high-quality protein.

Anchovies contain high levels of essential omega-3 fatty acids and protein, which help the body to repair and renew skin, bone, and muscle, and hold back the ravages of time. The protein in anchovies also helps regulate energy levels by reducing sugar cravings, making it an important player in effective metabolism and weight management. As oily fish is high in omega fatty acids and low in saturated fats, it is the perfect alternative to red meat. Anchovies support heart health, and also have a high B-vitamin profile. Two portions a week of anchovies, or any oily fish, has been shown to significantly reduce the risk of heart attacks, which increases as we grow older.

- The small bones in anchovies provide calcium to keep bones strong and the heart pumping efficiently.
- Selenium helps detoxify heavy metals, such as mercury and cadmium, that have an aging effect.
- Vitamins B_3 and B_5 create energy in all cells to keep the body young.

Practical tips:
Fresh anchovies are hard to find but there are some anchovies that are more healthily preserved than others. Anchovies sold in jars are preserved in oil rather than salt, and marinated white anchovies (available in most delis and supermarkets) have a less intense flavor than canned ones.

DID YOU KNOW?

The strong flavor of anchovies makes them a common ingredient in many popular condiments, not just fish sauces but also Worcestershire sauce.

MAJOR NUTRIENTS PER 3½ oz/100 g ANCHOVIES

Calories	131
Total fat	4.84 g
EPA	0.54 g
DHA	0.91 g
Protein	20.35 g
Carbohydrate	0 mg
Fiber	0 mg
Vitamin B_3	14.02 mg
Vitamin B_5	0.65 mg
Calcium	147 mg
Selenium	36.5 mg

Anchovies with artichokes and herbs

SERVES 4

3½ oz/100 g preserved anchovies

14 oz/400 g artichoke hearts
  preserved in olive oil

3 oz/85 g sun-dried tomatoes in oil

½ tbsp white wine vinegar

2 tbsp coarsely chopped
  fresh parsley

1 tsp chopped fresh rosemary

1 oz/25 g Parmesan cheese,
  shaved (optional)

pepper

Method

1 Drain the anchovies and discard the preserving liquid.

2 Drain the artichokes, reserving the oil. Halve or quarter them as necessary, then arrange on a serving dish. Put 2 tablespoons of the artichoke oil in a skillet and add the anchovies. Heat and cook gently for 2 minutes, then remove the anchovies with a slotted spoon and arrange over the artichokes.

3 Drain the tomatoes, reserving the oil. Finely chop them, then scatter over the anchovies. Combine another 1 tablespoon of the artichoke oil with 1 tablespoon of the tomato oil, the vinegar, parsley, rosemary, and pepper.

4 Sprinkle the oil dressing over the platter and serve scattered with the Parmesan cheese, if using.

50 TROUT

Trout provides a package that safeguards joints, eyes, and brain from damage and keeps them working like new.

Omega-3 fatty acids are crucial players in mood and behavior regulation as they affect how we use the stabilizing brain chemicals serotonin and dopamine. Eating oily fish one to three times a week has also been shown to improve brainpower and slow down the loss in concentration, memory, and mental acuity associated with aging and stress. Of all the oily fish, trout is one of the least contaminated by mercury toxicity. Mercury is common in larger oily fish, such as tuna and swordfish, which can spend years accumulating this dangerous and aging substance.

- Contains pink astaxanthin, which supports good eye health and keeps the brain firing on all cylinders.
- Vitamin D is needed for an agile brain. Low levels are linked to depression and dementia.
- High levels of the B vitamins promote youthful vitality and increased energy levels.
- Omega-3 fatty acids lubricate joints to ensure pain-free agility.

Practical tips:
Trout can be bought both fresh and smoked. The fresh fish are easy to stuff with herbs and lemon and bake, and the smoked variety makes a good alternative to the stronger flavored salmon. This is an excellent choice of oily fish for people who are put off by a strong fishy flavor.

DID YOU KNOW?

Trout is a type of salmon, but unlike salmon, trout spends its life in freshwater streams and ponds rather than in salt water.

MAJOR NUTRIENTS PER 3½ oz/100 G FRESH TROUT

Calories	148
Total fat	6.61 g
EPA	0.2 g
DHA	0.53 g
Protein	20.77 g
Carbohydrate	0 mg
Fiber	0 mg
Vitamin B$_1$	0.35 mg
Vitamin B$_3$	4.5 mg
Vitamin B$_{12}$	7.79 mg
Vitamin D	155 IU

Smoked trout salad

SERVES 4

1 red bell pepper, halved
   and seeded

4 smoked trout fillets, about
   5½ oz/150 g each, skinned,
   any small bones removed,
   and flaked

4 scallions, trimmed and finely
   chopped

2 large chicory heads, halved,
   cored, and shredded

1½ tbsp Chinese rice vinegar

½ tbsp sunflower oil

2 tbsp chopped fresh parsley

radicchio leaves, rinsed and dried

salt and pepper

Method

1 Run a swivel-bladed vegetable peeler along the length of the cut edges of the bell pepper to make very thin slices. Chop the slices and put them in a bowl.

2 Add the trout, scallions, and chicory, tossing to mix together. Add 1 tablespoon of the vinegar, the oil, parsley, and salt and pepper and toss again, then add extra vinegar as required.

3 Cover and chill until ready to serve. Arrange the radicchio leaves on individual plates. Toss the salad again and adjust the seasoning, if necessary. Place a portion of salad on each plate of radicchio leaves and serve.

51

LIVE GREEK-STYLE YOGURT

Live Greek-style yogurt contains bacterial cultures that boost the immune system and keep the digestive system young and robust.

Greek-style yogurt contains less sugar and more protein than other yogurts as it is strained to remove the carbohydrate-rich whey. Its thickness leaves you fuller than more watery versions and the lower level of lactose (milk sugar) it contains makes it easier to digest. Eating live yogurt regularly has been shown to enhance immune responses and our resistance to disease.

- All yogurts help reduce "bad" LDL cholesterol, but only "live" yogurt also raises "good" HDL cholesterol levels, ensuring the arteries stay functioning youthfully.
- People who regularly eat yogurt increase their fat-burning capacity, which leads to weight loss—especially around the waist.
- An important vitamin B_{12} source for vegetarians that helps to prevent dry skin and premature aging, as well as Alzheimer's disease, heart disease, and diabetes.

Practical tips:
Always choose live yogurt as these contain the beneficial live cultures. If possible, buy from local health food stores or farmer's markets; these products will have their own natural bacteria, rather than bacteria that has been added in the production process. Avoid fruit-flavored yogurt as this contains added sugar, and instead sweeten with fruit or cinnamon. The creamy, fresh taste of Greek-style yogurt makes it a good alternative to milk, cream, sour cream, or crème fraîche in savory dishes.

DID YOU KNOW?

People have been making yogurt for around 5,000 years. However, yogurt wasn't commercially produced until 1919, in Barcelona.

MAJOR NUTRIENTS PER 3½ FL OZ/100 ML LIVE GREEK YOGURT

Calories	61
Total fat	3.25 g
Protein	3.47 g
Carbohydrate	4.66 g
Vitamin A	99 IU
Vitamin B_2	0.14 mg
Vitamin B_5	0.39 mg
Vitamin B_{12}	0.37 mcg
Choline	15.2 mg
Calcium	121 mg
Potassium	155 mg

Tzatziki

SERVES 4 (M)(D)(B)(H)(I)

1 small cucumber
1¼ cups live Greek-style yogurt
1 large garlic clove, crushed
1 tbsp chopped fresh mint or dill
salt and pepper

Method

1   Peel and coarsely grate the cucumber. Put in a strainer and
    squeeze out as much of the water as possible. Put the cucumber
    into a bowl.

2   Add the yogurt, garlic, and chopped mint (set aside a little as a
    garnish, if liked) to the cucumber and season with pepper. Mix well
    together and chill in the refrigerator for about 2 hours before serving.

3   Stir the cucumber and yogurt dip and transfer to a serving bowl.
    Sprinkle with salt and serve.

52

KEFIR

Although kefir is less well known than its cousin yogurt, its rejuvenating immune-enhancing properties are making it increasingly popular.

Adding kefir to the diet gives an extra dimension to the immune-supporting actions of fermented foods, such as yogurt, miso, and sauerkraut. It has been shown to have extremely positive effects in the digestive tract, where the balance of good and bad bacteria is the foundation of our ability to fight bacterial infection, viruses, and fungal overgrowths—all of which compromise our ability to stay youthful. Kefir has also been shown to actively destroy harmful invading bacteria, and is believed to slow the growth of certain tumors. One of the probiotic bacteria alive in kefir, *Lactobacillus casei*, is strong enough to fight off pneumonia.

- Kefir's smaller curds make it easier to digest than yogurt, which helps it in its task of removing aging toxins via the digestive system.
- Has all the protein and calcium benefits of milk but is easier to tolerate for people with mild lactose intolerance.
- Traditionally used by shepherds to boost energy, help relieve skin disorders, and promote longevity.

Practical tips:
You can hunt down kefir at good health food stores, or make it yourself from cultures available on the Internet. Kefir can also be made with coconut water or even just water (although the nutritional values listed on this page include the nutrients of milk). Use kefir as you would yogurt. It makes a great base for smoothies as the sour taste offsets fruit perfectly.

DID YOU KNOW?

Kefir is similar to yogurt, except the milk has been fermented with kefir grains. These grains are lumps of bacteria and yeast, which are held together by large sugar molecules.

MAJOR NUTRIENTS PER 3½ FL OZ/100 ML KEFIR

Calories	61
Total fat	Varies according to milk used
Protein	Varies according to milk used
Carbohydrate	Varies according to milk used
Calcium	120 mg
Potassium	150 mg
Zinc	0.36 mg

Blueberry smoothie

SERVES 2

heaping ⅓ cup kefir

heaping ⅓ cup water

scant 1 cup blueberries plus extra,
   for decoration

Method

1 Put the kefir, water, and blueberries into a food processor
   or blender and process until smooth.

2 Pour into glasses and top with whole blueberries.

53

GOAT CHEESE

Goat cheese is higher in calcium and lower in fat than cheese made from cow milk, making it better for bone strength and as a rejuvenating source of protein.

DID YOU KNOW?

The fat particles in goat milk are much smaller than those in cow milk, being closer in size to those in human milk. This is why goat milk is easier to digest and why there is no need for the homogenization process.

MAJOR NUTRIENTS PER 3½ oz/100 G GOAT CHEESE

Calories	364
Total fat	29.84 g
Omega-6 fatty acids	706 mg
Omega-9 fatty acids	6,098 mg
Protein	21.58 g
Carbohydrate	2.54 g
Vitamin A	1,464 IU
Vitamin D	22 IU
Vitamin B_1	0.07 mg
Vitamin B_2	0.68 mg
Vitamin B_3	1.15 mg
Choline	15.4 mg
Calcium	298 mg
Phosphorus	375 mg
Manganese	6.06 mg
Selenium	3.8 mcg

Cheese is especially valuable for vegetarians as an alternative to meat. Goat cheese tends to be more traditionally made than cow milk cheeses, so can contain fewer chemical additives and preservatives. Although it contains the same protein, casein, that is present in cow milk and may cause allergies, it takes a different form and is often more tolerated by people with digestive sensitivities. Goat cheese provides a type of saturated fat that is needed for nervous system communication and that is healthy when eaten in a diet that is also high in omega-3 and omega-6 fatty acids, such as those found in oily fish, nuts, and seeds.

- Contains phosphorus, manganese, vitamin B_3, and vitamin A, which all help to lock calcium into the bones, keeping them strong.
- The combination of protein with quality saturated fat can help prevent the sugar cravings that lead to premature aging of the skin, eyes, and organs.
- Goat milk is higher in vitamins B_1 and B_3 than cow milk. These B vitamins make energy to repair cells and boost vitality.

Practical tips:
Choose soft cheeses for less saturated fat, and cheeses from farm stores or markets for optimum nutritional benefits. Check the labels of well-known cheeses, such as feta, as they are sometimes made with cow milk. Cheeses may also be made with sheep milk, which is similar to goat milk in terms of lactose content.

Goat cheese, pear, and walnut salad

SERVES 4

9 oz/250 g dried penne

1 head radicchio, torn into pieces

1 iceberg lettuce, torn into pieces

½ cup chopped walnuts

2 ripe pears, cored and diced

2 oz/55 g arugula

4 tomatoes, cut into quarters

1 small onion, sliced

1 large carrot, grated

9 oz/250 g goat cheese, diced

salt and pepper

Dressing

2 tbsp lemon juice

5 tbsp extra virgin olive oil

1 garlic clove, chopped

3 tbsp white wine vinegar

Method

1 Bring a large pan of lightly salted water to a boil over medium heat. Add the pasta and cook according to the package directions. Drain the pasta thoroughly and refresh in cold water, then drain again and set aside to cool.

2 Put the radicchio and iceberg lettuce into a large salad bowl and mix together well. Top with the pasta, walnuts, pears, and arugula.

3 To make the dressing, mix the lemon juice, oil, garlic, and vinegar together in a small bowl. Pour the dressing over the salad ingredients and toss to coat the salad greens well. Add the tomato, onion, carrot, and goat cheese and toss together with 2 forks, until well mixed. Let the salad chill in the refrigerator for about 1 hour before serving.

54

FREE-RANGE EGGS

Eggs are a perfect protein source, containing all of the amino acids needed for the body to repair itself and stay young-looking.

MAJOR NUTRIENTS PER MEDIUM-SIZE EGG

Calories	65
Total fat	4.37 g
Monounsaturated fat	1.68 g
Omega-3 fatty acids	32.6 mg
Omega-6 fatty acids	505 mg
Omega-9 fatty acids	1,582 mg
Protein	5.53 g
Carbohydrate	0.34 g
Vitamin A	214 IU
Vitamin D	22 IU
Vitamin B_2	0.21 mg
Vitamin B_5	0.63 mg
Vitamin B_{12}	0.57 mcg
Vitamin K	0.1 mcg
Choline	110.5 mg
Iron	0.81 mg
Selenium	13.9 mcg
Zinc	0.49 mg
Lutein/Zeaxanthin	146 mcg

Eggs are ideally packaged to support new life, and so contain all the nutrients we need for growth: iron, zinc, vitamin A, vitamin D, the B vitamins, and omega-3 fatty acids. Many people avoid them because of their high cholesterol content, but the body can regulate this if the diet is low in sugar and saturated fat. Many studies show that egg consumption helps prevent chronic age-related conditions, such as coronary heart disease, loss of muscle mass, eye degeneration, hearing loss, and memory loss.

- Contain vitamin B_{12}, which helps combat fatigue, depression, and lethargy.
- Vitamin A and lutein ensure eye protection and continuing good sight.
- One of the few dietary sources of vitamins K and D, which work together to keep bones strong.
- Contain sulfur and lecithin, substances that help the liver with digestion and detoxification.

Practical tips:
Eggs are a truly useful pantry food. They can be cooked in many different ways, including poaching, scrambling, and boiling. Omelets or frittatas, loaded with healthy vegetables, can also be eaten cold as a snack at any time. Buy organic free-range as the chickens' feed gives these eggs a higher nutritional value, indicated by their deeper yellow yolk and richer taste.

Mixed herb omelet

SERVES 1

2 large eggs

2 tbsp milk

3 tbsp butter

*leaves from 1 fresh parsley sprig,
   chopped*

2 fresh chives, chopped

salt and pepper

1 fresh chervil sprig, for garnishing

fresh salad greens, for serving

Method

1 Break the eggs into a bowl. Add the milk and salt and pepper to taste, and quickly beat until just blended.

2 Heat an 8-inch/20-cm omelet pan or skillet over medium–high heat until very hot and you can feel the heat rising from the surface. Add 2 tablespoons of the butter and use a spatula to rub it over the bottom and around the side of the pan as it melts.

3 As soon as the butter stops sizzling, pour in the eggs. Shake the pan forward and backward over the heat and use the spatula to stir the eggs around the pan in a circular motion. Do not scrape the bottom of the pan.

4 As the omelet begins to set, use the spatula to push the cooked egg from the edge toward the center, so that the remaining uncooked egg comes in contact with the hot bottom of the pan. Continue doing this for 3 minutes, or until the omelet looks set on the bottom but is still slightly runny on top.

5 Put the chopped herbs in the center of the omelet. Tilt the pan away from the handle, so that the omelet slides toward the edge of the pan. Use the spatula to fold the top half of the omelet over the herbs. Slide the omelet onto a plate, then rub the remaining butter over the top. Garnish with the sprig of chervil and serve immediately, accompanied by fresh salad greens.

55 QUAIL'S EGGS

Weight for weight, quail's eggs contain even more nutrients and accessible protein than chicken's eggs, helping to repair and renew skin, bones, and muscles.

MAJOR NUTRIENTS PER 4 QUAIL'S EGGS

Calories	56
Total fat	4 g
Monounsaturated fat	1.56 g
Omega-6 fatty acids	338.4 mg
Omega-9 fatty acids	1,338 mg
Protein	4.68 g
Carbohydrate	0.16 g
Vitamin A	196 IU
Vitamin D	20 IU
Vitamin B_2	0.28 mg
Vitamin B_5	0.63 mg
Vitamin B_{12}	0.56 mcg
Choline	94.8 mg
Iron	1.32 mg
Selenium	11.6 mcg
Zinc	0.52 mg
Lutein/Zeaxanthin	132 mcg

Quail's eggs have a higher yolk-to-white ratio than chicken's eggs. This means that for their size you get a good dose of the yellow carotenoid lutein, which helps prevent damage to fats in your body. The brain, heart, skin, eyes, and liver are just a few of these fatty areas and they are very susceptible to damage, so protecting them from the aging effects of toxins is crucial to staying young. Quail's eggs have been used for hundreds of years in traditional Chinese medicine to help combat immune-compromising allergies, such as hay fever and asthma, and aging skin conditions, such as acne, psoriasis, and eczema.

- Vitamin D helps revitalize bone and brain, so a dietary source is especially important when we can't get it from sunlight in the winter.
- Choline helps brain function, keeping memory and concentration performing youthfully.
- High selenium, zinc, and vitamin A content provides antioxidant protection, preventing aging and supporting new skin growth.

Practical tips:
Quail's eggs can replace chicken's eggs in any dish, but their beauty lies in their miniature yolk and white, so simply boiling and slicing into a salad is the best option. They fall apart less easily than chicken's eggs and have a slightly richer, gamier flavor.

Quail's egg salad with a spicy seed topping

SERVES 4 AS AN APPETIZER OR SNACK (**S**)(**M**)(**B**)(**H**)(**I**)

24 fresh quail's eggs

2 oz/55 g mixed salad greens

8 black olives, pitted and sliced
into rounds

1 tbsp French dressing

pepper

Topping

⅓ cup blanched hazelnuts

1 tbsp cumin seeds

1 tbsp coriander seeds

3 tbsp sesame seeds

½ tsp ground sea salt

Method

1 Bring a large saucepan of water to a boil. Cook the quail's eggs for 3 minutes, then put into a strainer. Run under cold water until cooled, then peel.

2 To make the topping, lightly toast the hazelnuts and all the seeds in a dry skillet until you can smell the aroma (do not overtoast). Mix in the salt. Let cool for 5 minutes and then place in a mortar and pound with the pestle until you have a coarse sprinkling mixture.

3 Arrange the salad greens (tearing them as necessary) on 4 serving plates and sprinkle over the olives. Drizzle over the French dressing and arrange the eggs on top. Grind over some black pepper. Sprinkle the topping over the salad and serve.

GRAINS AND BEANS

These foods contain protein, carbohydrates, and fats. They are ideal for vegetarians, who should eat some of each every day to take on their portfolio of amino acids. The high fiber content of grains and beans also enables your body to clean out aging toxins and balance hormone levels to help you stay young.

(S) Skin, hair, and nails

(M) Mobility and strength

(D) Digestive/detoxification health

(B) Brain health

(H) Heart health

(I) Immunity-supporting antioxidant

56

BROWN BASMATI RICE

Brown basmati rice, with its longer grains, provides 20 percent more fiber than other types of brown rice, helping to remove more aging toxins from the body.

DID YOU KNOW?

Basmati means "the fragrant one" in Sanskrit. Its smell comes from the chemical 2-Acetyl-1-pyrroline, which also gives jasmine rice and white bread their distinctive aromas.

MAJOR NUTRIENTS PER ⅓ CUP UNCOOKED RICE

Calories	370
Total fat	2.92 g
Omega-6	1,000 mg
Protein	7.94 g
Carbohydrate	77.24 g
Fiber	3.5 mg
Vitamin B$_1$	0.4 mg
Vitamin B$_3$	5.09 mg
Vitamin B$_5$	1.49 mg
Vitamin B$_6$	0.51 mg
Choline	30.7 mg
Vitamin E	1.2 mg
Magnesium	143 mg
Iron	1.47 mg
Manganese	3.74 mg
Selenium	23.4 mg
Zinc	2.02 mg

Basmati is a superior rice, with long, brown whole grains that provide more of the nutritious hull and less of the starchy inner germ than other rice varieties. This also means it releases its complex carbohydrates into the bloodstream more slowly, sustaining energy levels for longer, regulating appetite, and reducing cravings for sweet and fattening foods. The hull contains all the healthy oils, including omega-6 fatty acids and vitamin E, vital for glowing skin and fertility. The B vitamins and zinc in basmati also support these actions.

- Contains choline, which is used to make the membranes of new cells, so keeping skin young and vital.
- Selenium is necessary for coenzyme Q-10 production, which acts like a spark plug in the cells, firing off energy for rejuvenation.
- Magnesium is a calming mineral that helps combat the aging effects of stress.
- Manganese is a critical component of the protective antioxidant enzyme superoxide dismutase.

Practical tips:

When cooking, follow the directions on the package as nowadays many brands do not need soaking or rinsing first. Bear in mind that brown rice can be stored for less time than white as it contains more nutrients for bacteria to grow on.

Kidney bean pilaf

SERVES 4

4 tbsp olive oil

1 onion, chopped

2 garlic cloves, finely chopped

scant 1 cup brown basmati rice

2½ cups low-salt vegetable stock

1 red bell pepper, seeded
    and chopped

2 celery stalks, sliced

8 oz/225 g cremini mushrooms,
    thinly sliced

15 oz/425 g canned red kidney
    beans, drained and rinsed

3 tbsp chopped fresh parsley,
    plus extra for garnishing

½ cup cashew nuts

salt and pepper

Method

1 Heat half the oil in a large, heavy-bottom saucepan. Add the onion and cook, stirring occasionally, for 5 minutes, or until soft. Add half the garlic and cook, stirring frequently, for 2 minutes, then add the rice and stir for 1 minute, or until the grains are thoroughly coated with the oil. Add the stock and bring to a boil, stirring constantly. Reduce the heat, cover, and simmer for 35–40 minutes, or until all the liquid has been absorbed.

2 Meanwhile, heat the remaining oil in a heavy-bottom skillet. Add the red bell pepper and celery and cook, stirring frequently, for 5 minutes. Add the mushrooms and the remaining garlic and cook, stirring frequently, for 4–5 minutes.

3 Stir the rice into the skillet. Add the beans, parsley, and cashew nuts. Season to taste and cook, stirring constantly, until piping hot. Transfer to a warmed serving dish, sprinkle with the extra parsley, and serve.

57

MILLET

This underrated nongluten grain provides high levels of hormone-balancing and skin-plumping omega-6 fatty acids.

Millet contains none of the sticky gluten found in wheat, oats, rye, and barley. This makes it easier to digest and less likely to set off inflammatory tendencies that cause conditions, such as eczema, asthma, acne, arthritis, osteoporosis, and irritable bowel syndrome. The omega-6 fatty acids present in millet also help to soothe these aggravating conditions. Omega-6 fatty acids are also vitally important for digestion, immunity, detoxification, and metabolism. Eating them stops us from craving more unhealthy and aging oils, fats, and sugars, and helps maintain healthy, youthful-looking skin, hair, and nails.

- The B vitamins and magnesium support the adrenal glands and help to prevent stress from aging the body prematurely.
- Contains vitamin B_3, which lowers high cholesterol and keeps our brains functioning positively.
- Both copper and manganese are needed to make the large amounts of the detoxifying enzyme superoxide dismutase that keeps your system youthful.
- Phosphorus plays a part in energy production in every cell; this enables new bone to form and fuels the DNA that drives renewal throughout the body.

Practical tips:
The most common type of millet sold is the pearl, hulled type, but a millet couscous made from the cracked grain is also available from good health food stores. Millet flakes can be made into oatmeal or added to granola.

DID YOU KNOW?

Millet was one of the first grains to be eaten, meaning that we are much more likely to be able to digest it and suffer less intolerance.

MAJOR NUTRIENTS PER ½ CUP UNCOOKED MILLET

Calories	378
Total fat	4.22 g
Omega-6	2,015 mg
Protein	11.02 g
Carbohydrate	72.85 g
Fiber	8.5 mg
Vitamin B_1	0.42 mg
Vitamin B_2	0.29 mg
Vitamin B_3	4.72 mg
Vitamin B_5	0.85 mg
Vitamin B_6	0.38 mg
Magnesium	114 mg
Phosphorus	285 mg
Manganese	1.63 mg
Copper	Trace

Millet oatmeal with apricot puree

SERVES 4

heaping 1 cup millet flakes
2 cups milk
pinch of salt
freshly grated nutmeg

Apricot puree

scant ¾ cup coarsely chopped
    plumped dried apricots
1¼ cups water

Method

1 To make the apricot puree, put the apricots into a saucepan and cover with the water. Bring to a boil, then reduce the heat and simmer, half covered, for 20 minutes until the apricots are very tender. Transfer the apricots, along with any water left in the saucepan, to a food processor or blender and process until smooth. Set aside.

2 To make the oatmeal, put the millet flakes into a saucepan and add the milk and salt. Bring to a boil, then reduce the heat and simmer for 5 minutes, stirring frequently, until cooked and creamy. To serve, spoon into 4 bowls and top with the apricot puree and a little nutmeg.

58

QUINOA

The best source of complete protein in the plant kingdom, quinoa provides all the necessary building blocks for age-defying skin, and bone and brain regeneration.

MAJOR NUTRIENTS PER ⅔ CUP UNCOOKED QUINOA

Calories	368
Total fat	6.07 g
Omega-6	2,977 mg
Protein	14.12 g
Carbohydrate	64.16 g
Fiber	7 mg
Vitamin B₁	0.36 mg
Vitamin B₂	0.32 mg
Vitamin B₃	1.52 mg
Vitamin B₅	0.77 mg
Vitamin B₆	0.49 mg
Folate	184 mg
Magnesium	197 mg
Iron	4.57 mg
Phosphorus	457 mg
Potassium	563 mg
Manganese	2.03 mg
Selenium	8.5 mcg
Zinc	3.1 mg

Most plant foods are lacking in one or more essential amino acid, meaning that vegetarians and vegans need to consider carefully what range of foods they eat in order to get the right spread for youthful health. Quinoa is an easy one-food solution, containing all the essential amino acids, and it also provides a good range of minerals and the B vitamins. These enable the protein content of quinoa to be used effectively, so that it can provide the vast amount of energy needed for the constant renewal of skin, hair, nails, teeth, bone, and organs. Quinoa is actually a seed, not a grain. As such, it is high in anti-inflammatory omega-6 fatty acids and is ideal for those people who cannot tolerate wheat or gluten.

- Contains phosphorus to make phospholipids in the brain and nervous system, which enable you to move and think youthfully.
- Potassium balances out the sodium in your diet, reducing bloating, puffiness, and high blood pressure.
- Zinc and selenium offer potent antioxidant protection from aging elements in your life, such as pollution, sunlight, and chemicals.

Practical tips:
Quinoa cooks in a similar way to rice. It has a pleasant, nutty flavor, and is delicious in Mexican and Indian meals. You can also make a great quinoa oatmeal, either from flakes or from the grain itself. Quinoa is versatile enough to be cooked in both sweet and savory dishes.

Tabbouleh

SERVES 4

1 cup quinoa

2½ cups water

10 vine-ripened cherry
  tomatoes, halved

3-inch/7.5-cm piece
  cucumber, quartered and sliced

3 scallions, finely chopped

juice of ½ lemon

2 tbsp extra virgin olive oil

4 tbsp chopped fresh mint

4 tbsp chopped fresh cilantro

4 tbsp chopped fresh parsley

salt and pepper

Method

1 Put the quinoa into a medium saucepan and cover with the water. Bring to a boil, then reduce the heat, cover, and simmer over low heat for 15 minutes. Drain if necessary.

2 Let the quinoa cool slightly before combining with the remaining ingredients in a salad bowl. Adjust the seasoning, if necessary, before serving.

59 BUCKWHEAT

Buckwheat contains a rich supply of youth-enhancing flavonoids, particularly rutin. These help to keep your circulation flowing freely and prevent varicose veins.

Buckwheat is technically a seed, not a grain, so it is an excellent source of fiber and energy for people who are intolerant to wheat and gluten. Whether you have an intolerance or not, reducing your wheat intake will take pressure off the body. Buckwheat is not only easier to digest than wheat but also more alkalizing, meaning that it helps all physical processes work as efficiently as possible, whatever your time of life. It is a particularly sustaining energy source and is recommended for diabetics as it releases its sugars slowly into the bloodstream. Buckwheat, like millet, also contains substances called nutrilosides that are essential in detoxification processes, helping rid the body of harmful, aging toxins.

- Contains lecithin, which helps break down fats in the liver and in the food that you eat, aiding detoxification and reducing cravings for fatty foods.
- Magnesium and potassium work together to ensure a healthy heart and strong bones for youthful mobility.
- Selenium produces both of the rejuvenating antioxidants glutathione and coenzyme Q-10.

Practical tips:
Buckwheat may be used as an alternative to rice. It can also be bought in flakes and made into oatmeal. Buckwheat flour makes excellent gluten-free crepes, which are traditional in Poland and Russia, and also eaten in France.

DID YOU KNOW?

Buckwheat is not related to wheat. It isn't even a grain, but a fruit seed, in the same family as rhubarb and sorrel.

MAJOR NUTRIENTS PER ⅔ CUP BUCKWHEAT

Calories	343
Total fat	3.4 g
Omega-6	1,052 mg
Protein	13.25 g
Carbohydrate	71.5 g
Fiber	10 mg
Vitamin B₂	0.43 mg
Vitamin B₃	7.02 mg
Vitamin B₅	1.23 mg
Vitamin B₆	0.21 mg
Folate	30 mcg
Magnesium	231 mg
Potassium	460 mg
Manganese	1.33 mg
Selenium	8.3 mcg
Zinc	2.4 mcg

Buckwheat and tomato casserole

SERVES 4　

2 tbsp olive oil

1 onion, chopped

2 garlic cloves, crushed

heaping 1 cup buckwheat

14 oz/400 g canned chopped
　tomatoes

½ tsp tomato paste

heaping 1 cup low-salt
　vegetable stock

1 tbsp chopped fresh sage,
　or ½ tbsp dried sage

pinch of dried chile flakes

¾ cup crumbled, drained feta
　cheese

salt and pepper

Method

1　Heat the oil in a deep skillet with a tight-fitting lid over medium–high heat. Add the onion and garlic and fry for 5 minutes. Add the buckwheat and stir around for 1 minute, until you can smell a "toasty" aroma.

2　Add the tomatoes, the tomato paste, stock, sage, chile flakes, and salt and pepper to taste, stirring to dissolve the tomato paste. Bring to a boil, stirring, then reduce the heat to low, cover the pan, and let simmer for 20–25 minutes, until the liquid has been absorbed and the buckwheat is tender.

3　Lightly stir in the feta cheese, re-cover the pan, and let the buckwheat stand for up to 20 minutes. Just before serving, lightly stir with a fork.

60

SPELT

The rich fiber content of spelt can help to manage weight fluctuations and keep you trim and active as you get older.

MAJOR NUTRIENTS PER ½ CUP SPELT

Calories	338
Total fat	2.43 g
Omega-6	1,193 mg
Protein	14.57 g
Carbohydrate	70.19 g
Fiber	10.7 mg
Vitamin B₁	0.36 mg
Vitamin B₃	6.84 mg
Vitamin B₅	1.07 mg
Vitamin B₆	0.23 mg
Magnesium	136 mg
Potassium	388 mg
Phosphorus	401 mg
Iron	4.44 mg
Manganese	2.98 mg
Selenium	11.7 mcg
Zinc	3.28 mg

Spelt has not been through the selective breeding undergone by its modern counterpart, wheat. This makes it lower in the potentially inflammatory and difficult to digest gluten that causes intolerances in so many people. Spelt is also higher in iron and vitamin K, both needed to ensure the health of our blood, the life force that carries oxygen and nutrients around the body to vitalize every single cell. It has higher levels of omega-6 fatty acids, too, which keep our cells flexible and are an important contribution to youthful skin. Omega 6 also supports the nervous system to ensure quick brain and muscle reactions.

- Selenium activates the thyroid hormones that keep you burning energy and calories to help you retain a slim and youthful figure.
- Fiber slows the rate at which you break down food, so stabilizes blood-sugar levels and helps you resist quick-fix foods that pile on weight.
- Manganese and vitamin B₃ help to produce insulin, another vital ingredient in the management of blood-sugar levels.

Practical tips:
Many spelt breads and crackers are now available in health food stores, and spelt can be used as a substitute for rice or potatoes. If you have a severe intolerance to wheat, however, it is advisable to avoid spelt as well, because the proteins in spelt are similar and may provoke the same reaction.

Three-grain risotto with squash and asparagus

SERVES 4

7 oz/200 g butternut squash
or other type of squash,
peeled, seeded, and cut
into 4 wedges

1 tsp olive oil

²/₃ cup finely chopped onion

1 tsp crushed garlic

¹/₃ cup three-grain risotto
mix (baldo rice, spelt, and
pearl barley—prepared mixes
are available on the Internet)

2½ cups low-salt vegetable stock

8 oz/225 g asparagus tips

2 tbsp finely chopped fresh
marjoram, plus extra
for garnishing

3 tbsp live Greek-style yogurt

2 tbsp finely chopped parsley

pepper

Method

1 Preheat the oven to 400°F/200°C. Spread out the squash wedges on a nonstick baking sheet and roast in the oven for 20 minutes, or until tender and golden brown.

2 Meanwhile, heat the oil in a medium saucepan over high heat, add the onion and garlic, and cook, stirring, until softened but not colored. Add the risotto mix and stir in half the stock. Simmer, stirring occasionally, until the stock has reduced in the pan. Pour in the remaining stock and continue to cook, stirring occasionally, until the grains are tender.

3 Cut three-quarters of the asparagus into 4-inch/10-cm lengths and blanch in a saucepan of boiling water for 2 minutes. Drain and keep warm. Cut the remaining asparagus into ¼-inch/5-mm slices and add to the risotto for the last 3 minutes of the cooking time.

4 Remove the risotto from the heat and stir in the marjoram, yogurt, and parsley. Season with pepper. Do not reboil.

5 To serve, spoon the risotto onto warmed serving plates and top with the squash wedges and asparagus. Garnish with marjoram.

61

RYE

Rye is an excellent alternative to wheat. Its lower gluten level means it has less potential to cause inflammation, which can slow the body down and make you feel old.

MAJOR NUTRIENTS PER ¾ CUP DARK RYE FLOUR

Calories	325
Total fat	2.22 g
Omega-6	958 mg
Protein	15.91 mg
Carbohydrate	15.91 g
Fiber	23.8 mg
Vitamin B$_1$	0.32 mg
Vitamin B$_2$	0.25 mg
Vitamin B$_3$	4.27 mg
Vitamin B$_5$	1.46 mg
Vitamin B$_6$	0.44 mg
Magnesium	160 mg
Iron	4.97 mg
Manganese	6.06 mg
Selenium	18 mcg
Zinc	5.04 mg
Lutein/Zeaxanthin	210 mcg

Rye contains generous amounts of minerals and fiber, both of which help the body to clear out damaging toxins and harmful cholesterol. It also provides approximately 20 percent of its calories from protein and a good mix of the amino acids necessary to rebuild and repair all our body structures, from skin to teeth. The levels of protein and fiber in rye ensure that it has a very low glycemic index score of 26, meaning it releases its sugars very slowly into the bloodstream, which gives us energy over a long period without wanting to eat more. Good levels of magnesium, vitamin B$_6$, and zinc support this action by helping the body to produce the hormone insulin and use sugars efficiently.

- Lutein and zeaxanthin offer carotenoid antioxidant protection from damage to our brains, hearts, liver, and skin.
- High magnesium content helps us to make the body proteins we need, and so build skin and bone like new.
- Vitamin B$_5$ holds back the aging effects of stress.

Practical tips:
Dark rye is denser and more nutritious than medium and light types. The average supermarket loaf uses medium rye, which is often mixed with wheat to make the bread fluffier, so check labels. Pumpernickel is a dark rye flour and is used to make the pure rye bread of the same name.

Rye bread

MAKES 1 LARGE LOAF (S) (M) (D) (B) (H)

3¼ cups dark rye flour

scant 1⅔ cups bread flour,
    plus extra for dusting

2 tsp salt

2 tsp light brown sugar

1½ tsp active dry yeast

scant 2 cups lukewarm water

2 tsp light olive oil, plus extra
    for brushing

1 egg white

Method

1 Sift the flours and salt together into a bowl. Add the sugar and yeast and stir to mix. Make a well in the center and pour in the lukewarm water and oil. Stir with a wooden spoon until the dough begins to come together, then knead with your hands until it leaves the side of the bowl. Turn out onto a lightly floured counter and knead for 10 minutes, until elastic and smooth.

2 Brush a bowl with oil. Shape the dough into a ball, put it in the bowl, and cover with a damp dish towel. Let rise in a warm place for 2 hours, until the dough has doubled in volume.

3 Brush a baking sheet with oil. Turn out the dough onto a lightly floured counter and punch down with your fist, then knead for an additional 10 minutes. Shape the dough into a ball, put it on the prepared baking sheet, and cover with a damp dish towel. Let rise in a warm place for an additional 40 minutes, until the dough has doubled in volume. Meanwhile, preheat the oven to 375°F/190°C.

4 Beat the egg white with 1 tablespoon of water in a bowl. Bake the loaf in the preheated oven for 20 minutes, then remove from the oven and brush the top with the egg white glaze. Return to the oven and bake for an additional 20 minutes. Brush the top of the loaf with the glaze again and return to the oven for an additional 20–30 minutes, until the crust is a rich brown color and the loaf sounds hollow when tapped on the bottom with your knuckles. Transfer to a wire rack to cool.

62

WHEAT SPROUTS

Sprouted grains contain more than twice the dietary fiber of the usual grain, making them even more effective at eliminating aging toxins.

The fiber in wheat contains inulin, a substance that feeds the beneficial bacteria in our digestive tract, supporting our digestive and immune systems. Sprouting the wheat breaks down a lot of the substances, such as lectins, that many people are allergic or intolerant to, and the growing seed is also fueled by enzymes that help its digestion in our bodies. Because our ancestors ate wheat in this form, we are more adapted to it and it causes our bodies less stress, and thus reduces the speed of aging. Modern wheat is prone to cause constipation and mucus congestion, especially if it is eaten too often.

- Contains magnesium, needed for 300 body functions that keep you vital, including a quick brain and a healthy pumping heart.
- Choline helps the liver do its job and also ensures you get as much energy as possible from your food.
- Betaine supports all body processes and promotes youthful heart health, detoxification, and the creation of new cells.

MAJOR NUTRIENTS PER 1 CUP WHEAT SPROUTS

Calories	198
Total fat	1.27 g
Omega-6	531 mg
Protein	7.49 mg
Carbohydrate	42.53 g
Fiber	1.1 mg
Vitamin C	2.6 mg
Vitamin B$_1$	0.23 mg
Vitamin B$_3$	3.09 mg
Vitamin B$_5$	0.95 mg
Vitamin B$_6$	0.27 mg
Magnesium	82 mg
Iron	2.14 mg
Manganese	1.86 mg
Selenium	42.5 mcg
Zinc	1.65 mg
Choline	Trace
Betaine	Trace

Practical tips:
Sprouted wheat bread is available at good health food stores, with no added ingredients, making it suitable for people with yeast intolerance. Whole or blended sprouted wheat grains can be used in any whole wheat bread recipe, or you can try a Middle Eastern-style salad with sprouted wheat grains, onions, tomatoes, pine nuts, and herbs.

Wheat sprouts and garden vegetable salad

SERVES 4

4 small carrots, thinly sliced
1½ cups snow peas
2 cups small broccoli florets
6 scallions, chopped
12 cherry tomatoes, halved
3¾ cups fresh wheat sprouts,
    about 14 oz/400 g
1 handful fresh cilantro leaves,
    for serving

Dressing
3 tbsp extra virgin olive oil
juice of ½ lemon
salt and pepper

Method

1 Bring a saucepan of water to a boil and blanch or steam the carrots, snow peas, and broccoli for 2 minutes. Refresh under cold running water, and dry thoroughly in a clean dish towel or paper towels.

2 Place the vegetables in a salad serving bowl with the scallions and cherry tomatoes. Stir in the wheat sprouts.

3 To make the dressing, combine the olive oil, lemon juice, salt, and pepper in a small bowl. Pour over the salad and toss together. Scatter the cilantro leaves over to serve.

63 ALFALFA

Alfalfa is a well-known sprouted seed with fantastic detoxifying abilities that help your body remove harmful toxic metals.

Alfalfa has the capability to help us deal with the aluminum, mercury, lead, and other heavy metals that are present in the industrialized environment we share. This is mostly thanks to its chlorophyll content, the substance that plants use to create energy from the sun. Chlorophyll contains all of the essential amino acids that we need for correct liver function and blood vessel structure, including lysine, which has been shown to actively remove plaque from artery walls and destroy viruses, such as flu, herpes, and shingles. Alfalfa is also one of the richest sources of cholesterol-lowering saponins.

- Used in traditional Chinese and Indian medicines to treat digestive disorders, arthritis, and water retention.
- High vitamin A and beta-carotene content provides a natural defense against aging UV sun rays.
- Contains all the essential nutrients that you need from your food for a superior antiaging package.

Practical tips:
Alfalfa is one of the easiest seeds or beans to grow in a sprouting jar. You can buy both the jars and the seeds in good health food stores, or else buy it already sprouted. Always eat alfalfa raw. Try sprinkling liberally onto salads and in sandwiches as an addition to salad vegetables.

DID YOU KNOW?

The mature alfalfa plant is a huge crop in the United States, where it is included in cattle feed. Humans only eat the very young, sprouted seed, and we have used it medicinally for 1,500 years.

MAJOR NUTRIENTS PER 1⅓ CUPS ALFALFA

Calories	9.2
Total fat	0.28 g
Protein	1.6 g
Carbohydrate	0.84 g
Fiber	0.76 g
Vitamin C	3.28 mg
Vitamin A	62 IU
Vitamin B₃	0.19 mg
Vitamin B₅	0.22 mg
Vitamin K	30.5 mcg
Choline	5.76 mg
Beta-carotene	34.8 mcg
Calcium	12.8 mg
Magnesium	10.8 mg

Alfalfa reviver

SERVES 1–2

1 small zucchini

1 celery stalk

1½ cups baby leaf spinach

1⅓ cups alfalfa sprouts, plus extra
for garnishing

2 apples, peeled and cored

Method

1 Trim the zucchini and pack into the juicer with the celery.
Add the spinach and the alfalfa, then the apples. Juice all the
ingredients, then pour into glasses. Garnish with a few alfalfa
sprouts and serve.

64 CORN

The rich yellow color of corn derives from its high carotenoid levels, which provide protection against aging for the eyes, brain, skin, and heart.

DID YOU KNOW?

Also called maize, corn is native to Central America and Mexico. There is evidence that cornmeal was used by the Native Americans as long as 7,000 years ago, and the cereal in all its forms is still used widely today.

MAJOR NUTRIENTS PER ¾ CUP CORNMEAL

Calories	361
Total fat	3.86 g
Omega-6	1,706 mg
Protein	6.93 g
Carbohydrate	76.85 g
Fiber	7.3 g
Vitamin A	214 IU
Vitamin B₁	0.24 mg
Vitamin B₃	1.9 mg
Vitamin B₅	0.66 mg
Vitamin B₆	0.37 mg
Beta-carotene	97 mcg
Lutein/Zeaxanthin	1,355 mcg
Magnesium	93 mg
Potassium	315mg
Selenium	15.4 mcg
Zinc	1.73 mg

The carotenoids beta-carotene, lutein, and zeaxanthin are present in corn in an effective combination and amount, working alongside other antioxidants, vitamin A, and the minerals selenium and zinc to provide immunity and as protection against damaging inflammation. Corn also contains ferulic acid, which has been shown to be effective against tumors in the breasts and liver. Ferulic acid is used in sports to improve strength and increase lean muscle mass and, as an antioxidant, protects against the damaging free radicals produced when you expend more energy. Ferulic acid also protects membranes, so it strengthens the skin and fights the signs of aging.

- Contains vitamin A and lutein, which protect the eyes from age-related macular degeneration.
- Rich in omega-6 fatty acids that support immunity and anti-inflammatory actions to ensure good health.
- A nongluten grain that releases its sugars extremely slowly, ensuring sustained youthful energy.

Practical tips:
Corn tortillas are a useful alternative to bread for people who want to reduce the wheat and yeast content in their diet. Check labels, though, as the softer tortillas may still contain wheat. Polenta, the Italian version of cornmeal, makes a good alternative to rice or couscous, and can be used as the basis of wheat-free cakes.

Red bell pepper cornbread

MAKES ONE 1 LB/450 G LOAF (S) (M) (I)

*1 large red bell pepper, seeded
   and sliced*

*heaping 1 cup fine cornmeal
   or polenta*

heaping ¾ cup all-purpose flour

1 tbsp baking powder

1 tsp salt

2 tsp raw brown sugar

heaping 1 cup milk

2 eggs, lightly beaten

3 tbsp olive oil, plus extra for oiling

Method

1 Preheat the oven to 400°F/200°C. Lightly oil an 8 x 4 x 2-inch/20 x 10 x 5-cm loaf pan. Arrange the red bell pepper slices on a baking sheet and roast in the preheated oven for 35 minutes, until tender and the skin begins to blister. Set aside to cool slightly, then peel away the skin.

2 Meanwhile, mix the cornmeal, flour, baking powder, salt, and sugar together in a large mixing bowl. Beat the milk, eggs, and oil together in a separate bowl or pitcher and gradually add to the flour mixture. Beat with a wooden spoon to make a thick, smooth, batterlike consistency.

3 Finely chop the red bell pepper and fold into the cornmeal mixture, then spoon into the prepared pan. Bake in the preheated oven for 30 minutes, until lightly golden. Let cool in the pan for 10 minutes, then run a knife around the edge of the pan and turn the loaf out onto a wire rack to cool. To keep fresh, wrap the loaf in foil or seal in a plastic bag.

65

LENTILS

With 26 percent of their calorific value coming from protein, lentils are an important staple in any vegetarian diet, creating strong skin, nails, and hair.

MAJOR NUTRIENTS PER ½ CUP DRIED LENTILS

Calories	352
Total fat	1.06 g
Protein	25.8 g
Carbohydrate	60.08 g
Fiber	30.5 g
Vitamin B$_1$	0.87 g
Vitamin B$_2$	0.21 mg
Vitamin B$_3$	2.61 mg
Vitamin B$_5$	2.14 mg
Vitamin B$_6$	0.54 mg
Folate	479 mcg
Magnesium	122 mg
Iron	7.54 mg
Manganese	1.33 mg
Selenium	8.3 mcg
Zinc	4.78 mg

Lentils also provide a good dose of insoluble fiber, which is the type that stays undigested in our digestive tract and works hard to clean out the intestines, absorbing and taking away the aging toxins that the liver has detoxified. Insoluble fiber also keeps digestion regular and prevents the constipation that can lead to high cholesterol, poor hormone regulation, and bloating. It has even been shown to reduce the risk of colon and rectal cancers. The other starchy fibers in lentils provide a high-quality compact energy source that your body can draw on slowly and steadily, without the danger of blood-sugar highs or lows, or the weight gain these fluctuations often cause.

- One of the best vegetable sources of iron, lentils ensure that youth-giving oxygen keeps circulating in the body.
- Antioxidant minerals zinc and selenium work in the liver to protect against aging toxins.
- The B vitamins, folate, and magnesium help support youthful heart function.
- Manganese helps calcium move into bone and keep it strong, so helps to prevent osteoporosis.

Practical tips:
If you find lentils difficult to digest, soak them overnight before cooking and discard the water. This will remove many of the starches that cause problems. Lentils have a short cooking time. Add to vegetable soups or stews to provide a protein boost.

Spiced lentils with spinach

SERVES 4–6

2 tbsp olive oil

1 large onion, finely chopped

1 large garlic clove, crushed

½ tbsp ground cumin

½ tsp ground ginger

1¼ cups French green lentils

2½ cups low-salt vegetable stock

3½ oz/100 g baby spinach leaves

2 tbsp fresh mint leaves

1 tbsp fresh cilantro leaves

1 tbsp fresh parsley

lemon juice

salt and pepper

strips of lemon rind, for garnishing

Method

1 Heat the oil in a large skillet over medium heat. Add the onion and cook, stirring occasionally, for about 6 minutes. Stir in the garlic, cumin, and ginger and cook, stirring occasionally, until the onion starts to brown. Stir in the lentils. Pour in enough stock to cover the lentils by 1 inch/2.5 cm and bring to a boil. Reduce the heat and simmer for 20–30 minutes, until the lentils are tender.

2 Meanwhile, rinse the spinach leaves in several changes of cold water and shake dry. Finely chop the mint, cilantro leaves, and parsley.

3 If there isn't any stock left in the pan, add a little extra. Add the spinach and stir through until it just wilts. Stir in the mint, cilantro, and parsley. Adjust the seasoning, adding lemon juice and salt and pepper. Transfer to a serving bowl and serve, garnished with lemon rind.

66 ADZUKI BEANS

Adzuki beans are an excellent protein source. They also contain a healthy dose of soluble fiber, which keeps skin supple and nails and hair in tip-top condition.

The antioxidant properties of beans have long been overlooked. Studies in recent years have shown that their profile in this respect is similar to that of apples, berries, and red grapes. The red color of adzuki beans also provides rich helpings of protective flavonoids, especially catechins, which are also present in green tea, and proanthocyanidins. These are present in higher quantities in adzuki beans than in either soy or kidney beans. In combination with the fiber, protein, and good B-vitamin levels, the flavonoids make adzuki beans the perfect skin-conditioning food. This is why they are used in many antiaging skin creams and preparations.

- Contain folate that creates new growth in every cell to ensure the constant renewal of skin, nails, organs, and brain cells.
- Zinc also promotes cell growth and protects those cells from the effects of aging.
- Potassium prevents puffiness and bloating, and reduces high blood pressure.

Practical tips:
Pre-cooked, frozen adzuki beans are available in many good health food stores, and can be easily added to salads, soups, and stews. If cooking the beans yourself, adding a piece of kombu seaweed to the water, or changing the water several times, will remove some of the starches that can be difficult to digest.

DID YOU KNOW?

Adzuki beans are grown extensively through East Asia and the Himalayas, where they are commonly made into a sweet paste or ice cream.

MAJOR NUTRIENTS PER ½ CUP DRIED ADZUKI BEANS

Calories	329
Total fat	0.53 g
Protein	19.87 g
Carbohydrate	62.90 g
Fiber	12.7 g
Vitamin B$_1$	0.45 g
Vitamin B$_2$	0.22 mg
Vitamin B$_3$	2.63 g
Vitamin B$_5$	1.47 mg
Vitamin B$_6$	0.35 mg
Folate	622 mcg
Calcium	66 mg
Magnesium	127 mg
Potassium	1,254 mg
Phosphorus	381 mg
Iron	4.98 mg
Zinc	5.04 mg

Rainbow coconut drink with mango

SERVES 6

1 cup dried adzuki beans, soaked
   in water for 4 hours and drained
1 cup dried yellow split mung
   beans, soaked in water for
   3 hours and drained
3 cups canned unsweetened
   coconut milk
1 tsp salt
1 large ripe mango, peeled,
   seeded, and diced
sesame seeds, for decoration
crushed ice, for serving

Method

1 Put the adzuki beans with water to cover by 2 inches/ 5 cm in a medium saucepan and bring to a boil over high heat. Reduce the heat to medium and cook, stirring occasionally, for 2 hours, or until the water is completely absorbed by the beans and the beans are cooked through and tender.

2 Meanwhile, put the mung beans with water to cover by ¹/₂ inch/1 cm in a separate medium saucepan and bring to a boil over high heat. Reduce the heat to medium and cook, stirring occasionally, for 20–25 minutes, or until the water is completely absorbed by the beans. Let cool.

3 Put the coconut milk in a small saucepan and bring to a boil over high heat. Reduce the heat to medium–low and stir in the salt to dissolve. Let cool.

4 To assemble the drink, in individual parfait glasses, and in this order, layer 2–3 tablespoons each of coconut milk, adzuki beans, crushed ice, coconut milk, mung beans, crushed ice, coconut milk, and mango. Decorate with a light sprinkling of sesame seeds. Serve with a long-stem spoon.

67

MUNG BEANS

Mung beans are much easier to digest than other beans, and are a good source of cleansing fiber to counteract bloating and toxic buildup that can dull and age skin.

MAJOR NUTRIENTS PER ½ CUP DRIED MUNG BEANS

Calories	347
Total fat	1.15 g
Protein	23.86 g
Carbohydrate	62.62 g
Fiber	6.3 g
Vitamin B$_1$	0.62 mg
Vitamin B$_2$	0.23 mg
Vitamin B$_3$	2.25 mg
Vitamin B$_5$	1.91 mg
Vitamin B$_6$	0.38 mg
Folate	625 mcg
Choline	97.9 mg
Calcium	132 mg
Magnesium	189 mg
Potassium	1,246 mg
Phosphorus	367 mg
Iron	6.74 mg
Manganese	1.04 mg

Mung beans are an easy alternative to other starches in the diet. Swapping a grain for a bean such as these provides a carbohydrate energy source with the added bonus of extra protein. For vegetarians, mung beans also provide a good source of iron and the B vitamins for energy. Both are needed for good mental health, and low levels can result in fatigue, low mood, and poor skin, hair, and nail condition. The calcium, magnesium, and potassium in mung beans are all electrolyte minerals that we need in large amounts to ensure good heart, brain, and muscle function.

- Folate keeps skin renewed and vital. It also promotes fertility.
- Potassium keeps the body alkalized, meaning that you can get rid of aging toxins more effectively.
- Calcium and magnesium in balance help calm the nervous system and prevent stress from causing health problems and premature aging.
- Choline helps clear out any build up of fats from the liver, which can interfere with detoxification processes.

Practical tips:
Like lentils and other small beans, mung can be cooked from dried in about 20 minutes, making them perfect for adding to soups and stews. Canned mung beans are also available, but they should be washed thoroughly before use.

Mung bean soup

SERVES 6

heaping 1¼ cups peeled, split,
  dried yellow mung beans,
  soaked in water for 3 hours,
  then drained
4 cups canned unsweetened
  coconut milk
½ tsp salt
lightly toasted sesame seeds,
  for garnishing

Method

1 Put the mung beans with water to cover by ½ inch/ 1 cm in a medium saucepan and bring to a boil over high heat. Reduce the heat to medium and cook, stirring occasionally, for 20–25 minutes, or until the water is completely absorbed by the beans.

2 Transfer the beans to a fine mesh strainer set over a bowl. With the back of a spoon, press the beans against the side of the strainer. The result should be a very smooth paste.

3 Pour the coconut milk into a medium saucepan and bring to a gentle boil over medium heat. Add the mung bean paste and salt, and beat to a smooth consistency. Cook for 5 minutes, or until heated through.

4 Serve in individual bowls, scattered lightly with toasted sesame seeds.

68 BEAN SPROUTS

Sprouting is one of the most active times in a plant's life. You can benefit from this surge of vitality in terms of your own health and rejuvenation.

A sprouting seed heralds the emergence of a whole plant. This creates high levels of energy and involves a range of enzymes, the substances that speed growth and help us to detoxify when we eat them. These enzymes also make the beans easier to digest. Sprouting stimulates sugars to be turned into vitamin C as the plant begins to grow. The growing process involves combinations of amino acids, and a mix of bean sprouts, such as lentils, mung, and adzuki, therefore, provides a high-quality protein boost. Protein comprises 54 percent of the calories in soybean sprouts and 43 percent of the calories in mung bean sprouts.

- Sprouting makes beans more alkaline, which gives them improved detoxification capability.
- Rich phytoestrogen foods such as these bring balance to the hormones associated with energy, libido, and fertility.
- High folate content stimulates the regrowth of cells, which shows in glowing skin and strong nails.

Practical tips:
Sprouts are very easy to grow from beans, or you can buy a special sprouting mix from a health food store. Use a jar or a kit, and rinse the sprouts twice daily for freshness. Before eating, check the sprouts have a clean, fresh smell and wash thoroughly with filtered water. If you buy beans already sprouted, keep refrigerated and eat within two days. They should always be eaten raw.

DID YOU KNOW?

A sprouted bean is simply one that has started to grow a shoot. Any seed can be sprouted: mung bean, lentils, chickpea, and beetroot are a few examples. Most bean sprouts sold in supermarkets are mung bean sprouts.

MAJOR NUTRIENTS PER 1 CUP MUNG BEAN SPROUTS

Calories	30
Total fat	0.18 g
Protein	3.04 g
Carbohydrate	5.94 g
Fiber	1.8 g
Vitamin C	13.2 mg
Vitamin A	21 IU
Vitamin E	0.10 mg
Vitamin K	33 mcg
Vitamin B$_3$	0.75 mg
Vitamin B$_5$	0.38 mg
Folate	479 mcg
Potassium	149 mg

Bean sprout salad with sesame

SERVES 4

2 tbsp toasted sesame oil

1 large red bell pepper, seeded and
   thinly sliced

3 large garlic cloves, finely chopped

½-inch/1.5-cm piece fresh ginger,
   peeled and finely chopped

2 shallots, thinly sliced

heaping ¾ cup mung bean sprouts
   (or other bean sprouts of choice)

1 tbsp sesame seeds

1 handful fresh basil leaves

Dressing

1 tbsp rice wine vinegar

2 tsp good-quality honey

1 tbsp light soy sauce

1 tsp hot chili sauce

Method

1 Heat 1 tbsp sesame oil in a skillet and add the red bell pepper.
   Stir-fry over medium heat for 3–4 minutes, to soften.

2 Add the garlic, ginger, and shallots and stir-fry for 2 minutes.
   Remove from the heat and let cool.

3 To make the dressing, combine the remaining sesame oil with the
   vinegar, honey, soy sauce, and chili sauce in a small bowl. Put the
   bean sprouts into a serving bowl. Stir in the red bell pepper mixture,
   add the dressing and sesame seeds, and toss together. Just before
   serving, tear the basil leaves and stir through lightly.

69

TOFU

Tofu, or bean curd, is made from soybeans and is widely used in Asian cooking. It is one of the factors associated with Asians' better health in old age.

Soy protein is one of the few plant sources of complete protein, which means that it contains all of the essential amino acids that you can't make in the body and must obtain through your diet. This includes the amino acid tryptophan that is necessary for good mood and sleep, and crucial in combating the aging effects of daily stress. Soy is also a rich source of saponins and fiber and is, therefore, often recommended as part of a diet intended to lower cholesterol. Lignins in soy proteins have been found to stop the growth and spread of prostate cancer cells. They also contain phytoestrogens, specifically the isoflavones genistein and diadzein. These have been shown to lower the incidence of hormone-related prostate and breast cancers and the rate of osteoporosis.

- Enriched with calcium for strong bones and a robust heart.
- Contains iron and copper, which is used by red blood cells to transport oxygen and renew worn-out cells.
- Copper is needed to make collagen and elastin from the enzyme lysyl oxidase, ensuring firm and flexible blood vessels, bones, and joints.

Practical tips:
Tofu is available in three varieties: firm, soft, and silken. Each has a different texture and usage. Tofu can seem bland when first tried but it easily soaks up flavors. Silken tofu also makes a good protein addition to smoothies.

DID YOU KNOW?

Tofu was first made 2,000 years ago, in China. It was first written about in a poem called "Ode to Tofu" by Su Ping in AD 1500.

MAJOR NUTRIENTS PER 3½ oz/100 g TOFU

Calories	76
Total fat	4.78 g
Protein	8.08 g
Carbohydrate	1.88 g
Fiber	0.3 g
Vitamin B₃	0.2 mg
Calcium	350 mcg
Copper	0.19 mg
Iron	5.36 mg
Manganese	0.61 mg
Selenium	8.9 mcg
Tryptophan	0.13 g

Vegetable and tofu stir-fry

SERVES 2–3

8 oz/225 g firm tofu, drained and
   cut into bite-size pieces
1 tbsp peanut or light olive oil
2 scallions, chopped
1 garlic clove, finely chopped
8 baby corn cobs, halved
2 cups snow peas
4 oz/115 g shiitake mushrooms,
   thinly sliced
2 tbsp finely chopped fresh
   cilantro leaves

Marinade

2 tbsp dark soy sauce
1 tbsp Chinese rice wine
2 tsp good-quality honey
½ tsp Chinese five-spice powder
1 fresh red chile, seeded and
   finely chopped
2 scallions, finely chopped
1 tbsp grated fresh ginger

Method

1 Place all the marinade
   ingredients in a large, shallow,
   nonmetallic dish and stir to
   mix. Add the bite-size chunks
   of tofu and turn them over
   carefully to coat thoroughly
   in the marinade. Cover
   the dish with plastic wrap
   and leave the tofu in the
   refrigerator to marinate for
   2 hours, turning the chunks
   over once or twice.

2 Drain the tofu and set aside
   the marinade. Heat the oil in a
   preheated wok or large skillet.
   Add the tofu and stir-fry over
   medium–high heat for 2–3
   minutes, or until golden. Using
   a slotted spoon, remove the
   tofu from the wok and set
   aside. Add the scallions
   and garlic and stir-fry for
   2 minutes, then add the corn
   cobs and stir-fry for 1 minute.
   Add the snow peas and
   mushrooms and stir-fry for an
   additional 2 minutes.

3 Return the tofu to the wok
   and add the marinade. Cook
   gently for 1–2 minutes, or until
   heated through. Sprinkle with
   the chopped fresh cilantro and
   serve immediately.

70 MISO

Miso is one of the traditional foods of Japan, where it is associated with long life and good health.

Like sauerkraut, yogurt, and kefir, fermented foods that are enjoyed in many cultures, miso is associated with good digestive health because it feeds the beneficial probiotic bacteria present in the body. This supports toxin elimination and the absorption of nutrients to keep you looking and feeling young and healthy. Fermented foods also help the immune system, keeping in check overreactions that can lead to multiple sensitivities and inflammation, as seen in hay fever and skin problems. The soy variety of miso is also a useful vegetarian protein source.

- Contains tryptophan, needed for serotonin production, which encourages good mood and restorative sleep.
- Manganese makes the detoxifying antioxidant enzyme superoxide dismutase to help slow down the aging process.
- Vitamin K transports calcium around the body in support of good bone health and efficient blood clotting.
- Zinc-rich food that promotes optimal immune function and rapid healing, helping your skin look more youthful.

Practical tips:
Miso is salty, but a little goes a long way in terms of taste and mineral content. The paste is superior to the powdered form and can be used just as easily to make an instant, simple soup when mixed with boiling water. Add miso to boiled vegetables and ginger to make a heartier broth, which you can supplement with shrimp, chicken, or tofu.

DID YOU KNOW?

Most miso is the hatcho form made from soybeans, but it can also be produced from rice, barley, or wheat by adding a koji yeast mold that stimulates fermentation.

MAJOR NUTRIENTS PER 1 TBSP MISO

Calories	34
Total fat	1.03 g
Protein	2.01 g
Carbohydrate	4.55 g
Fiber	0.93 g
Vitamin B_1	0.02 mg
Vitamin B_2	0.04 mg
Vitamin B_3	0.16 mg
Vitamin B_5	0.06 mg
Vitamin B_6	0.03 mg
Vitamin B_{12}	0.43 mcg
Vitamin K	8.53 mcg
Iron	0.43 mg
Selenium	1.2 mcg
Zinc	0.44 mg
Manganese	0.3 mg

Miso soup

SERVES 4

4 cups water

2 tsp dashi granules

6 oz/175 g silken tofu, drained
    and cut into small cubes

4 shiitake mushrooms, finely sliced

4 tbsp miso paste

2 scallions, chopped

1 Put the water in a large pan with the dashi granules and bring to a boil. Add the tofu and mushrooms, reduce the heat, and let simmer for 3 minutes.

2 Stir in the miso paste and let simmer gently, stirring, until the miso has dissolved.

3 Add the scallions and serve immediately. If you let the soup stand, the miso will settle, so give the soup a thorough stir before serving to recombine.

5

HERBS AND FLAVORINGS

Nature's flavorings are the basis for many traditional medicines and we are only now beginning to understand how powerful they can be in the fight against time. Keep a range of herbs and spices in the pantry and experiment with flavors to ensure that you don't have to rely on sugar and salt for taste.

(S) Skin, hair, and nails

(M) Mobility and strength

(D) Digestive/detoxification health

(B) Brain health

(H) Heart health

(I) Immunity-supporting antioxidant

71

CHIVES

Chives belong to the allium family and provide the same protective sulfur compounds as garlic and onion. These foods work hard to keep you detoxified.

Chives have the same health benefits as garlic, but are slightly weaker. They contain the same potent sulfur substance sulfoquinovosyl diacylglycerol, which is also found in spinach, parsley, green tea, and carrots, and which has been shown to stop the action that makes cancer cells proliferate. These foods also have antifungal and antibacterial properties, which help keep your digestive tract free from the elements affecting health and digestion, so preventing debilitating gas, bloating, and constipation. Because they are antiviral, too, they reduce the viral load that threatens the body's stocks of youthful energy and vitality.

- Contain the energy-producing nutrients vitamin C, citric acid, malic acid, and glutamic acid.
- Immune-supporting antioxidant power comes from vitamin C, beta-carotene, quercetin, and ferulic acid.
- Aid circulation in support of heart health so that it can pump revitalizing nutrients to all parts of the body.

Practical tips:
Chives are easy to grow. Keep a plant handy on a kitchen windowsill so you can add them to fish, potatoes, and soups. As they have a mild flavor, they can be easier to include in the diet than their cousin, garlic. They are particularly tasty when added to soft cheeses and with herring or other cured fish.

DID YOU KNOW?

Chives are grown in gardens to repel unwanted insects that feed off plants, and also to attract the bees that pollinate them.

MAJOR NUTRIENTS PER ½ oz/15 G CHIVES

Calories	30
Total fat	0.73 g
Protein	3.27 g
Carbohydrate	4.35 g
Fiber	2.5 g
Vitamin C	58.1 mg
Vitamin A	4,353 IU
Vitamin K	212.7 mcg
Beta-carotene	2,612 mcg
Lutein/Zeaxanthin	323 mcg

Herb salsa

MAKES ABOUT 1½ CUPS

3-inch/7.5-cm piece cucumber
2 tsp salt
6 scallions, finely chopped
2 celery stalks, finely chopped
1 green bell pepper, peeled,
*   seeded, and finely chopped*
⅔ cup live Greek-style yogurt
1 tbsp shredded fresh marjoram
1 tbsp chopped fresh parsley
1 tbsp chopped fresh chives

Method

1 Peel the cucumber very thinly and cut lengthwise into quarters. Scoop out and discard the seeds. Finely chop the flesh, put in a nonmetallic strainer, and sprinkle with the salt. Let drain for 15–20 minutes, then rinse thoroughly and drain well. Put in a small bowl.

2 Add the scallions, celery, and green bell pepper to the bowl and mix well. Add the yogurt and stir well before adding all the herbs. Stir again, then spoon into a serving dish. Lightly cover and let stand in a cool place, but not the refrigerator, for 30 minutes to let the flavors develop.

72

GREEN TEA

The Chinese and Japanese have long understood the health attributes of green tea, and view it as an important part of their heart, energy, and skin regimes.

The leaves of the tea plant *Camellia sinensis* are loaded with catechins, which have been found to have natural antioxidant, antibacterial, and antiviral properties, thereby protecting against cancer and helping to lower cholesterol and regulate blood clotting. One such compound, epigallocatechin gallate (EGCG), is able to penetrate the cells and protect the crucial DNA that the body relies on to replicate cells and combat the damage caused by aging. EGCG also prevents cancer cells from forming and can help reduce the severity of allergies by blocking the body's response.

- Green tea may also act as a weight loss aid by helping to burn fat and regulate blood-sugar and insulin levels.
- Contains quercetin, a bioflavonoid (plant chemical) that reduces inflammation and helps control food allergies.
- Catechins promote liver detoxification, so assists in the removal of aging toxins and promotes glowing skin.

Practical tips:
Changing from black tea or coffee to green tea, which will still give you a boost, will lower your total intake of caffeine and its aging effects. Different varieties have different strengths and taste. Genmaicha is a particularly palatable Japanese blend, with a nutty taste from the toasted brown rice that has been added to it.

DID YOU KNOW?

Green tea leaves are the dried leaves of the tea plant, while black, "normal" tea is fermented. The fermentation process makes black tea much higher in caffeine: roughly 50 mg a cup compared to 5 mg for green tea.

MAJOR NUTRIENTS PER 1 CUP BREWED GREEN TEA

Calories	approx* 2
Total fat	0 g
Protein	0 g
Carbohydrate	Negligible
Fiber	0 g
Catechins	3.75 g

*can vary greatly between varieties and strength of brew

Green tea and yellow plum smoothie

SERVES 2

1 green tea bag
1¼ cups boiling water
1 tsp good-quality honey, to taste
(optional)
2 ripe yellow plums, halved
and pitted

Method

1 Put the tea bag in a teapot or heatproof pitcher and pour over the boiling water. Let steep for 7 minutes. Remove and discard the tea bag. Let cool, then chill in the refrigerator.

2 Pour the chilled tea into a food processor or blender. Add the honey, if using, and plums, and process until smooth.

3 Serve at once.

73 CHAMOMILE

Chamomile tea is known as a soothing sleep aid. It also supports good digestion and immunity through lowering the stress levels that contribute to premature aging.

Drinking chamomile tea raises the body's levels of glycine, a compound that you use to make sleep-inducing neurotransmitters (brain chemicals). Its ability to calm the nervous system explains why it is able to relieve muscle spasms and headaches. Chamomile also raises levels of hippuric acid, the substance present in cranberries and blueberries that fights infection and helps stave off colds. Drinking chamomile tea regularly helps regulate digestive problems, such as stomach cramps, irritable bowel syndrome (IBS), and, because it has a mildly laxative effect, constipation.

• Contains the antioxidant flavonoids quercetin and apigenin for youthful heart and skin.
• Used chamomile tea bags can be placed on the eyes to reduce puffiness, swelling, and dark circles.
• Has anti-inflammatory and cholesterol-lowering properties that contribute to the prevention of age-related diseases.

Practical tips:
Chamomile tea, or manzanilla, is made by steeping the flowers and leaves of German chamomile (*Matricaria recutita*) in boiling water for 10–15 minutes. It can be bought easily as tea bags, but for more potency, buy the fresh plant and brew in a teapot. Experiment with strength to your taste and add a little honey, if necessary. It is best drunk in the evening as it acts as a mild sedative. Those who are allergic to ragweed should avoid as chamomile is in the same family.

DID YOU KNOW?

The ancient Egyptians used chamomile to alleviate premenstrual syndrome and the associated headaches and cramps.

MAJOR NUTRIENTS PER 1 CUP BREWED CHAMOMILE TEA

Calories	2
Total fat	0 g
Protein	0 g
Carbohydrate	0.47 g
Fiber	0 g

Chamomile tea with orange peel

SERVES 1

heaping 1 tsp dried or 2 tsp fresh
   chamomile flowers
1 piece fresh orange rind (no pith)
1 tsp good-quality honey

Method

1 Put the chamomile flowers and orange rind in an individual teapot.
   Pour over boiling water and stir. Let steep for 5 minutes.
2 Pour through a strainer into a serving mug and stir in the honey.
   Drink hot, or chill in the refrigerator and drink cold with ice.

74

CILANTRO

Cilantro, the leaves of the coriander plant, can help rid the body of the dangerous and aging toxic metals that pollute your environment, such as lead, mercury, and aluminum.

In our industrialized society, we are continually exposed to toxic metals. Our bodies need help to eliminate these safely and prevent a buildup, with its associated symptoms of insomnia, anxiety, depression, poor memory, and skin complaints. Research has shown that urinary excretion of mercury and aluminum increases after eating cilantro. These poisons are, therefore, moved out of the brain and central nervous system, where they can cause most damage. Cilantro has also been shown to result in a lower buildup of toxins in bone (toxins can displace essential calcium and age the skeleton), and in the blood (toxins can displace iron).

- Carotenoids add to the detoxifying profile of cilantro, protecting the liver against the harmful toxins it has to process.
- Its fragrant volatile oils are antimicrobials, which help to destroy immune-stressing invaders.
- Vitamins A and C together with an abundance of plant chemicals help to renew skin, brain, and bone.

Practical tips:
Cilantro needs to be bought fresh or grown on a plant as they quickly lose their aroma once dried or frozen. Their flavor is best enjoyed when eaten raw, so add at the end of cooking or as a generous garnish. They also work well in larger quantities as a salad green and as the main herb in a pesto sauce.

DID YOU KNOW?

In some areas of Europe, cilantro is called the "anti-diabetic plant." Studies show that it increases insulin to reduce blood-sugar levels.

MAJOR NUTRIENTS PER ⅓ CUP CHOPPED CILANTRO

Calories	3.5
Total fat	0.08 g
Protein	0.32 g
Carbohydrate	0.55 g
Fiber	0.42 g
Vitamin C	4.05 mg
Vitamin A	1,023 IU
Vitamin K	46.5 mcg
Beta-carotene	589.5 mcg
Lutein/Zeaxanthin	130 mcg

Carrot, orange, and cilantro salad

SERVES 4

1lb 2 oz/500 g carrots, coarsely
    grated
4 scallions, finely shredded
2 oranges
⅓ cup raisins
3 tbsp chopped fresh cilantro

Dressing

3 tbsp extra virgin olive oil
3 tbsp orange juice
2 tsp lemon juice
½ tsp ground cumin
½ tsp ground coriander
salt and pepper

Method

1 Place the carrot and scallions in a large bowl and toss gently to mix. Using a serrated knife, remove all the peel and pith from the oranges, then cut into segments between the membranes. Gently toss the orange segments into the bowl with the raisins and chopped cilantro.

2 To make the dressing, put all the ingredients into a small screw-top jar and shake until well blended.

3 Pour the dressing over the carrot salad and toss thoroughly. Cover with plastic wrap and chill in the refrigerator for 30 minutes. Season with salt and pepper. Serve.

75 LICORICE ROOT

Licorice is used by practitioners of alternative medicine as an adrenal support, safeguarding you from fatigue and the aging damage caused by stress.

The herb licorice is adaptogenic, which is the modern term for a "tonic." This means that it regulates body functions, in this case how you react to stress, as it affects the way your brain sends information to your adrenal glands. Licorice mimics the stress hormone cortisol and so supports energy, metabolism, and appropriate immune response. It is used extensively to treat digestive ailments as it supports the mucus membranes that coat the digestive tract wall, effectively soothing the digestive system and acting as a mild laxative. It also inhibits the bacteria *Helicobacter pylori*, which is responsible for stomach ulcers.

DID YOU KNOW?

Licorice is one of the most important herbs in Chinese medicine. It is believed to increase energy and help other herbs work together.

MAJOR NUTRIENTS PER 1 CUP BREWED LICORICE TEA

There are no nutrients listed in the standard reference, the USDA Database, at this time.

- Contains isoflavones that regulate sexual hormones, encouraging vitality, and may help to prevent cancer.
- Protects the liver from toxins and cholesterol from damage, which are both crucial to staying young.
- Powerful antiviral containing 10 antioxidant and 25 antifungal compounds to keep you healthy.

Practical tips:
Use the fresh root or herbal tea bags to make an energizing tea. Do not drink after 2 p.m. if you have problems sleeping. Licorice bars make a good alternative to chocolate, although they are usually sweetened (and contain wheat). Licorice capsules should be taken only under the supervision of a health professional. Avoid licorice if you have high blood pressure.

Licorice root and ginger tea

SERVES 1

1 tsp licorice root chips

1 level tsp finely chopped
fresh ginger

water

Method

1 Put the licorice chips and ginger into an individual teapot. Pour over boiling water and stir. Let steep for 5 minutes.

2 Pour through a strainer into a serving mug. Drink hot, or chill in the refrigerator and drink cold with ice.

76

CINNAMON

Cinnamon contains a chemical that mimics the hormone insulin, helping you to use sugars correctly for energy and prevent aging inflammation and weight gain.

This chemical (methylhydroxychalcone polymer, or MHCP) also stimulates the production of glycogen, the form of sugar that you store in muscles and the liver for those times when you need maximum energy, such as during exercise or when under stress. Its presence means that you don't crave fattening and aging refined sugars and can regulate your energy better. Cinnamon also prevents sugars in the bloodstream from damaging tissues and DNA, which can lead to inflammation and be extremely aging. Cinnamon is a superior sweetener for food, and an excellent flavoring for candies and desserts. When it is eaten, the brain receives a message that it has absorbed something sweet, but there is no damaging sugar surge in the bloodstream.

- Has a reputation as an aphrodisiac. Simply smelling cinnamon has been shown to improve brain reactions and memory.
- A teaspoon of cinnamon has the same antiaging antioxidant power as ½ cup of blueberries or a cup of pomegranate juice.
- Kills microbes and yeasts that upset digestion and immunity.

Practical tips:
Seasoning a high sugar or refined carbohydrate food with cinnamon lessens its damaging effects. Buy in stick form or ground, and check it has the sweet smell as this means it is fresh. The sticks keep for longer but the powder is stronger. Cinnamon may help relieve colds and flu when added to hot honey and lemon tea.

DID YOU KNOW?

Cinnamon was regarded as a gift fit for kings in ancient cultures. It has many mentions in the Old Testament, the first being when Moses uses it as a holy anointing oil.

MAJOR NUTRIENTS PER 2 TBSP GROUND CINNAMON (CASSIA)

Calories	37
Total fat	0.19 g
Protein	0.60 g
Carbohydrate	12.08 g
Fiber	7.96 g
Vitamin C	0.57 g
Vitamin A	44 IU
Calcium	150 mg
Manganese	2.62 mg

Star anise and cinnamon rub

MAKES ¼ CUP   (D) (B) (I)

2 tbsp whole star anise

1 tbsp black peppercorns

1 tsp light brown sugar

2 tsp salt

heaping 1 tsp ground cinnamon

Method

1 Put the star anise and peppercorns in an electric grinder and grind briefly until crushed to a coarse powder. Don't process or grind for too long, otherwise the spices will become oily. Stir in the sugar, salt, and cinnamon.

2 Rub the mixture thoroughly into meat, poultry, fish, or seafood a few hours before cooking.

3 Put in a shallow dish, cover tightly, and chill in the refrigerator until required.

77

GINGER

Ginger increases circulation, thins the blood, and is an anti-inflammatory. It supports the health of the heart, joints, and brain, keeping them youthful.

Numerous studies have shown that ginger lowers blood-cholesterol levels by intervening in its production. It thins the blood by reducing the stickiness of blood platelets, in much the same way as garlic. This action has been shown to reduce the risk of atherosclerosis—the formation of plaque on arteries—and to help prevent heart disease. Ginger has also been shown to help the transportation of "bad" LDL cholesterol to the liver, where it can be broken down and eliminated. A very strong antioxidant, ginger actually contains more than 12 constituents with a higher antioxidant potential than vitamin C.

- Used extensively for digestive problems, this zesty ingredient also kills off harmful bacteria to keep you healthy and feeling young.
- Shown to help prevent age- and stress-related diseases, including cancer, diabetes, ulcers, strokes, and arthritis.
- Enhances the body's use of serotonin, our happy mood and socialization neurotransmitter.
- Positive effect on circulation is a boost for young-looking skin.

Practical tips:
Even though the powdered spice is available, it is better to buy the fresh ginger. It stores well when refrigerated or frozen. Add a few slices to hot water with lemon as a cleansing drink first thing in the morning, or make into tea with cinnamon. Chop up roughly and add to stir-fries or curries.

DID YOU KNOW?

Related to turmeric and cardamom, ginger has been used in traditional Chinese medicine for 2,500 years. It is a sialagogue, which means it makes swallowing easier by stimulating saliva production.

MAJOR NUTRIENTS PER ⅜-INCH/8-MM PIECE FRESH GINGER

Calories	12
Total fat	0.11 g
Protein	0.27 g
Carbohydrate	2.66 g
Fiber	0.3 g
Vitamin C	2.4 mg
Potassium	62 mg

Stir-fried fresh crab with ginger

SERVES 4

3 tbsp peanut oil

2 large fresh crabs, cleaned,
  broken into pieces, and legs
  cracked with a cleaver

1½-inch/4-cm piece fresh ginger,
  cut into thin strips

3½ oz/100 g scallions, chopped
  into 2-inch/5-cm lengths

2 tbsp light soy sauce

pinch of white pepper

Method

1 In a preheated wok or deep saucepan, heat 2 tablespoons of the oil
   and cook the crab over high heat for 3–4 minutes. Remove from the
   wok and set aside.

2 In a clean wok or deep saucepan, heat the remaining oil, add the
   ginger, and stir until fragrant. Add the scallions, then stir in the
   crab pieces. Add the soy sauce and pepper. Cover and simmer
   for 1 minute and serve immediately.

78

TURMERIC

In terms of therapeutic health, turmeric is as important in the kitchen as its close cousin ginger, with a similar reputation for antiaging and disease prevention.

Turmeric has long been used in traditional Chinese medicine and traditional Indian Ayurvedic medicine as a remedy for joint problems, digestive problems, menstrual irregularities, and liver complaints. Statistics show that Indian levels of heart disease, and inflammatory conditions, such as arthritis, and cancer are much lower than in the West, and this is probably due to the enormous amounts of turmeric in the Indian diet. The active compound in turmeric, curcumin, has also been shown to help prevent multiple sclerosis, Alzheimer's disease, ulcers, skin complaints, carpal tunnel syndrome, and most digestive disorders. Much of this action is due to its ability to move harmful and aging toxins out of the body.

- Used in skin preparations as an anti-inflammatory and as a natural sunscreen to help avoid aging skin damage.
- It has antiseptic and antibacterial properties that support healing and promote youthful immunity.
- Contains specific cholesterol-lowering properties that promote optimal heart and brain function.

DID YOU KNOW?

The anti-inflammatory effects of turmeric have been favorably compared to prescription medications, such as hydrocortisone and phenylbutazone.

MAJOR NUTRIENTS PER 2 TBSP GROUND TURMERIC

Calories	53
Total fat	1.48 g
Protein	1.12 g
Carbohydrate	9.73 g
Fiber	3.16 g
Vitamin C	3.88 mg
Potassium	378 mg

Practical tips:

Following the Indian example, regular turmeric-laden curries are recommended if you want to benefit from its properties. However, it is now common in supplement form as it can be difficult to digest. As a supplement, it is often combined with bromelain from pineapples or piperine from black pepper to aid absorption.

Chickpea, almond, pea, and turmeric rice

SERVES 4

2 tbsp light olive oil
1 small onion, finely chopped
1 yellow or orange bell pepper,
  seeded and finely chopped
1 garlic clove, finely chopped
heaping 1 cup brown basmati rice
1 tbsp turmeric
3 cups low-salt
  vegetable stock
14 oz/400 g canned
  chickpeas, drained
heaping ¾ cup slivered almonds
1 cup small cooked peas

Method

1 Heat the oil in a large pan and cook the onion and bell pepper over medium heat until soft and tinged golden brown. Add the garlic and cook, stirring, for 1 minute.

2 Add the rice and stir for another 1 minute to coat with the oil, then add the turmeric and stir again. Pour in the stock and stir well. Bring to a boil, then simmer over low heat, covered, for 20 minutes.

3 Add the chickpeas, almonds, and peas and cook for an additional 5 minutes, or until the rice is tender and all of the stock has been absorbed. Transfer to a warmed serving dish and serve.

79

CLOVES

Cloves are associated with infusing the cold winter with warmth. Their warming property is the key to their ability to relieve aches and pains in the muscles and joints.

Cloves contain the active compound eugenol in sufficient quantities to be effective in detoxifying the harmful and aging pollutants that we take on from the environment. This is the substance used in dental preparations, such as mouthwashes, throat sprays, and toothpastes, as it both reduces bacteria in the mouth and has a mildly anaesthetic effect on the sensitivities that cause pain. As mouth infections are associated with heart disease, this is an important antiaging consideration. Studies have also shown that eugenol can reduce inflammation. If you eat cloves as part of an existing healthy diet, you will be helping to combat inflammatory symptoms like joint pain, skin flare-ups, and headaches, and reduce the level of "bad" LDL cholesterol in your body.

- The flavonoids kaempferol and rhamnetin offer youth-retaining antioxidant properties.
- Clove oil is used traditionally to treat acne and rashes, and to heal scars after burns and injuries, keeping skin looking young.

Practical tips:
Cloves are included in the curry spice mix garam masala and in the spiced tea chai. They are often mixed with cinnamon and cumin to provide warmth and comfort, especially in winter. Cloves can be added to hot water, honey, and lemon to make a delicious drink that is also an effective remedy for colds or flu. To spice up further, add ginger and cinnamon.

DID YOU KNOW?

Cloves are pressed into oranges at Christmas to make fragrant pomanders, and have also been used in incense.

MAJOR NUTRIENTS PER 2½ TBSP CLOVES

Calories	48.5
Total fat	3.04 g
Protein	0.89 g
Carbohydrate	9.18 g
Fiber	5.13 g
Vitamin C	12.12 mg
Vitamin K	22.27 mcg
Calcium	96.9 mg
Potassium	165 mg
Iron	13 mg
Manganese	4.5 mg

Chicken noodle soup with cloves and star anise

SERVES 4–6

2 skinless free-range chicken
   breasts
8 cups water
1 onion, unpeeled, halved
1 large garlic clove, halved
1-cm/½-inch piece fresh ginger,
   peeled and sliced
4 black peppercorns,
   lightly crushed
4 cloves
2 star anise
1 carrot, peeled
1 celery stalk, chopped
6–8 baby corn, cut in half
   lengthwise and chopped
2 scallions, finely shredded
4 oz/115 g dried rice vermicelli or
   Udon noodles
salt and pepper

Method

1 Put the chicken breasts and water in a pan over high heat and bring to a boil. Reduce the heat to its lowest setting and let simmer, skimming the surface until no more foam rises. Add the onion, garlic, ginger, peppercorns, cloves, star anise, and a pinch of salt, and simmer for 20 minutes, or until the chicken is tender and cooked through. Meanwhile, grate the carrot along its length on the coarse side of a grater so you get long, thin strips.

2 Strain the chicken, reserving about 5 cups stock, but discarding any flavoring solids. (At this point you can let the stock cool and refrigerate overnight, so any fat solidifies and can be lifted off and discarded.) Return the stock to the rinsed-out pan with the carrot, celery, baby corn, and scallions and bring to a boil. Boil until the baby corn are almost tender, then add the noodles and continue boiling for 2 minutes.

3 Meanwhile, chop the chicken and add to the pan and continue cooking for about 1 minute longer until the chicken is reheated and the noodles are soft. Add seasoning to taste.

80 PAPRIKA

Paprika is dried and powdered capsicum (bell pepper). It offers the same circulation-enhancing action as chile, helping your skin to stay looking young.

Paprika has been used traditionally to promote heart health, and has been shown to reduce "bad" LDL cholesterol. It is said to create heat in the body without burning or irritating, which increases circulation and ensures that invigorating oxygen and nutrients are distributed effectively around the whole body, including the heart. Like turmeric and cumin, paprika is high in salicylic acid, which forms the basis of aspirin. A single highly spiced curry can actually provide more than is contained within an aspirin pill. This explains the anti-inflammatory actions of these spices, which help keep joints mobile and the skin clear.

- Contains more protective vitamin C than lemon juice by weight, which is retained during drying and cooking.
- Increases saliva production, so promoting good digestion and the absorption of nutrients that fight aging.
- Helps reduce the bacterial infections that put stress on the body and age us prematurely.

Practical tips:
Store paprika away from light and get it out of the pantry only when you need to use it, as it loses color and flavor quickly when exposed. This also applies to the cooking process, so add it as close to the end of cooking as possible (unless you are making goulash). Don't be fooled by its mild taste in the package: paprika increases in strength and flavor when heated.

DID YOU KNOW?

Paprika has been used as a coloring in cosmetics for centuries, and some zoos have been known to add it to the flamingos' food to enhance their pink color.

MAJOR NUTRIENTS PER 2 TBSP GROUND PAPRIKA

Calories	43
Total fat	1.94 g
Protein	2.21 g
Carbohydrate	8.36 g
Fiber	5.61 g
Vitamin C	10.66 mg
Vitamin B$_3$	2.29 mg
Vitamin B$_6$	0.60 mg
Vitamin A	396 IU
Vitamin E	4.47 mg
Potassium	351 mg
Iron	3.53 mg
Zinc	0.60 mg
Beta-carotene	4,156 mcg
Lutein/Zeaxanthin	1,973 mcg

Goulash

SERVES 4

4 tbsp light olive oil

1 lb 7 oz/650 g braising steak,
    cut into 1-inch/2.5-cm cubes

2 tsp whole wheat flour

2 tsp paprika

1¼ cups low-salt beef stock

3 onions, chopped

4 carrots, diced

1 large potato or 2 medium
    potatoes, diced

1 bay leaf

½–1 tsp caraway seeds

14 oz/400 g canned chopped
    tomatoes

2 tbsp sour cream or live
    Greek-style yogurt

salt and pepper

Method

1 Preheat the oven to 325°F/170°C. Heat half the oil in a large,
   flameproof casserole. Add the beef and cook over medium heat,
   stirring frequently, until browned all over. Reduce the heat and stir
   in the flour and paprika. Cook, stirring constantly, for 2 minutes.
   Gradually stir in the stock and bring to a simmer.

2 Heat the remaining oil in a heavy-bottom skillet. Add the onions
   and cook over low heat, stirring occasionally, for 5 minutes,
   until softened. Stir in the carrots and potato and cook for a few
   additional minutes. Add the bay leaf, caraway seeds, and tomatoes.
   Season with salt and pepper.

3 Transfer the vegetable mixture to the casserole, stir well, then cover
   and cook in the oven for 2½ hours, until the meat is tender.

4 Remove and discard the bay leaf. Spoon into individual bowls and
   top with sour cream. Serve immediately.

81 HORSERADISH

Horseradish contains all of the benefits of its detoxifying cousins broccoli and cabbage. It is regarded as an aphrodisiac because it is stimulating and revitalizing.

Like all members of the brassica family, horseradish contains glucosinolates, which protect against the growth of tumors. These also support a particular liver detoxification process that regulates estrogen and progesterone, supporting women during all phases of life, and good prostate health in men. Specifically in horseradish, two types of glucosinolates, sinigrin and gluconasturtiin, provide the pungent taste that has been traditionally used for its heating properties. As well as adding fire to our food, horseradish stimulates immune cells and metabolism, kills off harmful bacteria, and strengthens the heart.

- The fresh root is high in vitamin C, which is a circulation booster, bringing youthful zing to the entire body.
- Naturally antibacterial and antiparasitic, so keeps the body safe from the unwanted elements in the food we eat.
- Improves breathing—which increases the amount of revitalizing nutrients taken to the body cells—by bringing up mucus and opening the airwaves.

Practical tips:
Horseradish usually comes prepared as a condiment, in jars. These products vary in quality so check the labels for added sugar or additives that will negate the health benefits. Horseradish can be freshly grated from the root. This will produce a more pungent taste, which gives a satisfying kick to homemade mackerel pâté.

....

DID YOU KNOW?

Grated horseradish should be used immediately or mixed in vinegar. Otherwise, upon exposure to heat and air it will darken, become unpleasantly bitter, and lose its pungency.

....

MAJOR NUTRIENTS PER 1 TBSP PREPARED HORSERADISH

Calories	7.2
Total fat	Trace
Protein	0.17 g
Carbohydrate	1.69 g
Fiber	0.49 g
Vitamin C	3.73 mg
Potassium	36.9 mg

Horseradish sauce

SERVES 6–8

6 tbsp creamed horseradish sauce

6 tbsp sour cream or live Greek-style yogurt

Method

1 In a small serving bowl, mix the horseradish sauce and sour cream together. Serve the sauce with roast beef, or with smoked fish, such as trout or mackerel.

82

WASABI

Wasabi is a strong natural antiparasitic, which helps us to enjoy omega-3-rich oily fish without the damaging consequences of a parasite infection.

Wasabi is a hotter, Asian version of horseradish. The hot vapors come from the isothiocyanates it contains. Its pungency is the secret weapon that can kill off a whole host of microbes, which we ingest perfectly naturally along with the various foods that we eat. As these microorganisms can compromise our digestion, immune system, and nervous system—affecting potentially all the systems of the body—to stay youthful and vibrant we need to employ continual defenses from nature's clever chemical pantry, such as wasabi.

- Related to broccoli, cabbage, and horseradish, with the same power to help the liver eliminate aging toxins.
- The isothiocyanates support youthful heart health, helping reduce the risk of stroke and heart attack.
- Anti-inflammatory action that boosts the youthful functioning of the joints and lungs.

Practical tips:
Dyed horseradish is sometimes served in Japanese restaurants in place of wasabi. It will contain the beneficial properties of horseradish, but also the potentially unhealthy chemicals of the green dye. Check that you are being served the real thing, and buy good-quality wasabi for use when cooking at home. Always use fresh wasabi and store it carefully as it will lose color and pungency quickly when exposed to air.

DID YOU KNOW?

Wasabi and its pungent vapors are at the center of research into the development of a sensory fire alarm for the deaf.

MAJOR NUTRIENTS PER 1 TSP WASABI PASTE

Calories	5.5
Total fat	Trace
Protein	0.24 g
Carbohydrate	1.18 g
Fiber	0.39 g
Vitamin C	2.09 mg
Potassium	28.4 mg

Daikon salad with a wasabi dressing

SERVES 4

8-inch/20-cm piece of daikon
½ cucumber
handful of baby spinach leaves,
    chopped
3 red radishes, sliced into thin
    rounds
a few leaves of Chinese cabbage,
    cut into thin strips
1 tbsp sunflower seeds
2 tsp white sesame seeds,
    lightly toasted

Wasabi dressing

4 tbsp rice vinegar
2 tbsp grapeseed oil
1 tsp light soy sauce
1 tsp wasabi paste
½ tsp good-quality honey
salt, to taste

Method

1 Shred the daikon using the finest setting on a mandolin or a very
   sharp knife. If you are using a knife, then cut the daikon into long,
   thin slices and cut each slice along its length as finely as you can.
   Rinse under cold water, then drain well.

2 Cut the cucumber in half lengthwise, and use a teaspoon to scoop
   out the seeds. Peel and slice in the same way as the daikon.

3 Place the sliced daikon and cucumber in a salad bowl with the
   chopped spinach. Add the sliced radishes and Chinese cabbage.

4 Place the ingredients for the dressing in a small bowl and stir to mix.
   Pour the dressing over the salad, toss gently to mix, and sprinkle
   with the sunflower seeds and the toasted sesame seeds.

83 BLACK PEPPER

Black pepper kick-starts our enjoyment of the foods it garnishes, and stimulates revitalizing beta-endorphins to have a positive effect on mood and boost

The spicy taste of black pepper comes from its ingredient piperine, which has recently been understood to assist in the absorption of nutrients, such as the energizing B vitamins and the immune-supporting antioxidants selenium and beta-carotene. It also supplements the anti-inflammatory and anticancer actions of the chemical curcumin, found in turmeric, by making it easier to absorb. The essential oils in black pepper are made of terpenes, such as limonene, also found in citrus fruits, and pinene, found in pine trees, that help prevent cancer, regulate heartbeat, and are antibacterial.

- Source of the mineral chromium, which promotes blood-sugar balance and good weight management.
- Strengthens membranes to help prevent varicose veins and keep skin firm and young.
- Believed to have antidepressant qualities, so encourages a youthful, positive, and motivated attitude.

Practical tips:
Black peppercorns have more nutrients than white peppercorns. Both are prepared from unripe pepper berries, but the white peppercorns have their skins removed. Buy the whole corns and invest in a good grinder for fresh ground and best-tasting pepper. Keep in a sealed glass container in a cool, dark place.

DID YOU KNOW?

Black peppercorns are not in the same family as bell peppers or chile, but the explorer Christopher Columbus assumed that this was the case when he came across them in Haiti.

MAJOR NUTRIENTS PER 2 TBSP BLACK PEPPERCORNS

Calories	38
Total fat	0.48 g
Protein	1.64 g
Carbohydrate	9.72 g
Fiber	3.98 g
Vitamin C	3.15 mg
Calcium	85.2 mg
Magnesium	29.1 mg
Potassium	189 mg
Manganese	0.84 mg
Chromium	Trace

Black pepper-crusted monkfish

SERVES 4

3 tbsp cracked black peppercorns

sea salt

1 lb 5 oz/600 g monkfish fillet,
    cubed

1 tbsp light olive oil

Sauce

1 tbsp light olive oil

1 shallot, finely chopped

1 garlic clove, finely chopped

3 tbsp white wine

heaping ⅓ cup thick plain live
    yogurt

1 level tsp cornstarch

2 tbsp coarse-grain mustard

2 tbsp chopped fresh dill

Method

1 Combine the cracked peppercorns with a little flaked sea salt and
   press the mixture into the monkfish pieces to coat.

2 To make the sauce, heat the oil in a small skillet. Add the shallot
   and stir-fry over medium heat for 3 minutes, until softened. Add the
   garlic and stir-fry for another 1 minute. Add the wine and cook until
   evaporated. Stir in the yogurt and cornstarch and bring to a simmer,
   then add the mustard, dill, and a little salt.

3 Heat the oil in a skillet until very hot. Add the monkfish cubes
   and cook for 3 minutes, turning during cooking so that each side
   is cooked. The fish is ready when the pieces are just firm when
   pressed. Remove with a slotted spoon and drain on paper towels.
   Serve with the sauce.

84

CARDAMOM

Like ginger, cardamom has a strong,
soothing effect on the digestive tract.
It helps you to digest a meal fully and
receive all of its rejuvenating nutrients.

The strong aromas of herbs and spices are testament to the
medical strength of their volatile oils. Many cultures have long
relied on their inclusion in the diet to ward away illness and
promote longevity. Generally speaking, they achieve this by helping
circulation, cleansing, and digestion and contributing to blood-
sugar balance. Cardamom has a particularly cleansing effect on
the digestive tract, and is traditionally used to treat stomach gripes
and pains, dysentery, and the constipation that can lead to toxic
buildup, high cholesterol, and hormonal problems.

- The oils help clear mucus from the throat, nose, and chest that
  can lead to aging inflammation.
- Helps clear out the kidneys to reduce fluid retention and maintain
  a clear, youthful-looking complexion.
- Chewing cardamom helps prevent the infections of teeth and
  gums that are linked to heart disease.

Practical tips:
Cardamom pods can be added to sweet and pungent dishes, but
use only a few as their strength can be overwhelming. Tea made
from the crushed seeds (you can reuse ones that you have cooked
with) is a traditional remedy for depression, and can be combined
with cinnamon to help alleviate a sore throat or hoarseness. The oil
of cardamom is recommended to massage away muscle tension.

DID YOU KNOW?

Cardamom has been used
as an antidote for scorpion
and snake bites in South
Asia, where it is a common
flavoring. It is also used
frequently in Nordic cuisine
and in Middle Eastern
candies, coffee, and tea.

**MAJOR NUTRIENTS
PER 2 TBSP CARDAMOM
SEEDS**

Calories	47
Total fat	1 g
Protein	1.614 g
Carbohydrate	10.27 g
Fiber	4.2 g
Vitamin C	3.15 mg
Calcium	57.45 mg
Magnesium	34.35 mg
Potassium	167.85 mg
Iron	2.09 mg
Manganese	4.2 mg

Spiced basmati rice

SERVES 4–6

heaping 1 cup brown or white
    basmati rice
2 tbsp ghee or peanut oil
5 green cardamom pods, bruised
5 cloves
2 bay leaves
½ cinnamon stick
1 tsp fennel seeds
½ tsp black mustard seeds
scant 2 cups water
1½ tsp salt
2 tbsp chopped fresh cilantro
pepper

Method

1 Rinse the rice in several changes of water until the water runs clear, then let soak for 30 minutes. Drain and set aside until ready to cook.

2 Melt the ghee in an ovenproof casserole or large saucepan with a tight-fitting lid over medium–high heat. Add the spices and stir for 30 seconds. Stir the rice into the casserole so the grains are coated with ghee. Stir in the water and salt and bring to a boil.

3 Reduce the heat to as low as possible and cover the casserole tightly. Simmer, without lifting the lid, for 8–10 minutes, until the grains are tender and all the liquid is absorbed.

4 Turn off the heat and use 2 forks to mix in the cilantro. Adjust the seasoning, if necessary. Re-cover the pan and let stand for 5 minutes.

85

MUSTARD

The pleasing heat of mustard illustrates its ability to stimulate the circulation, so that youth-giving nutrients and oxygen are distributed to all parts of the body.

The mustard seed is an excellent source of nutrients. As a member of the illustrious antiaging family of brassicas, which includes broccoli and cabbage, it contains glucosinolates and isothiocyanates that help prevent cancerous growths, especially hormone-related breast and prostate cancer. It also contains substances called mucilages that soothe the digestive tract wall and help the protective mucous lining stay intact. This lining allows nutrients into the system but keeps out aging elements, such as toxins, bacteria, and viruses. Mucilages also bulk out stools, inducing a mild laxative effect that supports cleansing digestion.

- Very high source of the mineral selenium, a potent antioxidant that keeps skin looking young.
- A digestive stimulant that facilitates optimum absorption of rejuvenating nutrients.
- Anti-inflammatory properties support smooth, blemish-free skin and supple joints.

Practical tips:
Mustard can be bought as a paste, when the ground seeds have been combined with water, or as a powder. Its health benefits decrease significantly if it is not used quickly, and the powder should always be stored in a dark, airtight container. To make up a whole-grain mustard, simply add vinegar to the seeds.

DID YOU KNOW?

Dating back to 3,000 BC, mustard is one of our oldest medicinal foodstuffs. Its name comes from the Latin *mustum* meaning "new wine."

MAJOR NUTRIENTS PER 4 TSP MUSTARD SEEDS

Calories	76
Total fat	3.28 g
Protein	3.91 g
Carbohydrate	4.21 g
Fiber	1.83 g
Vitamin C	1.06 mg
Vitamin B$_3$	0.71 mg
Selenium	31.21 mcg

Spicy fish curry

SERVES 4–6

3 tbsp peanut or coconut oil

1 tbsp black mustard seeds

12 fresh curry leaves or
  1 tbsp dried

6 shallots, finely chopped

1 garlic clove, crushed

1 tsp ground turmeric

½ tsp ground coriander

¼–½ tsp chili powder

5 oz/140 g creamed coconut,
  grated and dissolved in 1½
  cups boiling water, or 1½ cups
  canned coconut milk

1 lb 2 oz/500 g skinless, boneless
  white fish, such as monkfish or
  cod, cut into large chunks

1 lb/450 g large raw shrimp,
  shelled and deveined

finely grated rind and juice of 1 lime

salt

lime wedges, for garnishing

Method

1 Heat the oil in a karahi, wok, or large skillet over high heat. Add the mustard seeds and stir them around for about 1 minute, or until they jump. Stir in the curry leaves.

2 Add the shallots and garlic and stir-fry for about 5 minutes, or until the shallots are golden. Stir in the turmeric, coriander, and chili powder and continue stir-frying for about 30 seconds.

3 Add the creamed coconut. Bring to a boil, then reduce the heat to medium and cook, stirring, for about 2 minutes.

4 Reduce the heat to low, add the fish, and simmer for 1 minute, stirring the sauce over the fish and very gently stirring it around. Add the shrimp and continue to simmer for 4–5 minutes, until the fish flesh flakes easily and the shrimp turn pink and curl.

5 Add half the lime juice, then taste and add more lime juice and salt to taste. Sprinkle the lime rind over, garnish with lime wedges, and serve.

86 RED WINE

Red wine is an important contributor to the age-defying Mediterranean diet. Enjoyed in moderation, it offers excellent heart-protecting properties.

The high antioxidant action of red wine comes from a substance called resveratrol, found in red grape skins in much higher amounts than in any other food. The major action of resveratrol means that drinking red wine regularly in moderation—less than 2 units a day—can make blood platelets less sticky and help blood vessels stay youthfully open and flexible. These are both important considerations in regulating blood pressure and, therefore, cutting the risk of heart disease. Drinking red wine has been estimated to add a year to life expectancy, especially if drunk only with food and while incorporating the other youth-promoting components of the Mediterranean diet: plenty of vegetables, fruits, olive oil, and garlic.

• Resveratrol is an effective agent in disease prevention.
• It has also been shown to have a potent anti-inflammatory action, supporting clear, smooth skin and trouble-free joints.
• Cabernet Sauvignon in particular has been shown to help improve the memory deterioration shown in Alzheimer's disease.

Practical tips:
Straying above the recommended 1 drink a day for women and 2 drinks a day for men soon negates the benefits of red wine. Quality is also key: the deeper the red, the higher the antioxidant count. The greatest amounts are found in Merlot, Cabernet Sauvignon, and Chianti grapes. Rioja and Pinot Noir offer moderate amounts, while the least benefit is derived from Côtes du Rhône.

DID YOU KNOW?

Sipping red wine slowly may increase the blood levels of resveratrol by 100 times, because it is absorbed much better through the mouth than the digestive system.

MAJOR NUTRIENTS PER 4 FL OZ/125 ML RED WINE

Calories	95
Total fat	0 g
Protein	0.07 g
Carbohydrate	2.87 g
Potassium	145.6 mg

Honey-glazed red cabbage with golden raisins

SERVES 6

2 tbsp butter

1 garlic clove, chopped

1 medium head red cabbage,
*   shredded*

heaping ¾ cup golden raisins

1 tbsp good-quality honey

heaping ⅓ cup red wine

heaping ⅓ cup water

Method

1 Melt the butter in a large saucepan over medium heat. Add the garlic and cook, stirring, for 1 minute, until slightly softened.

2 Add the cabbage and golden raisins, then stir in the honey. Cook for an additional 1 minute. Pour in the wine and water and bring to a boil. Reduce the heat, cover, and simmer gently, stirring occasionally, for 45 minutes, or until the cabbage is cooked. Serve hot.

87 MOLASSES

Molasses has long been used as a health supplement. It is an excellent source of revitalizing minerals, which explains its rich, dark color.

MAJOR NUTRIENTS PER 1 TBSP MOLASSES

Calories	43.5
Total fat	Trace
Protein	0 g
Carbohydrate	11.2 g
Fiber	0 g
Vitamin B₃	0.14 mg
Vitamin B₅	0.12 mg
Vitamin B₆	0.1 mg
Choline	1.99 mg
Calcium	30.75 mg
Magnesium	36.3 mg
Potassium	219 mg
Iron	0.71 mg
Manganese	0.22 mg
Selenium	2.67 mcg

Molasses is high in a substance called uridine, also found in tomatoes and sardines, which has been shown to have as strong an antidepressant effect as commonly prescribed SSRI antidepressive medicines, such as Prozac. Uridine helps the action of omega-3 fatty acids, making chemical reactions in the brain happen more easily. This is assisted by the presence of the B vitamin choline, which forms new brain connections, keeping the mind young. Baking with molasses can enhance a treat food and significantly reduce its refined sugar content. Simply replacing half the sugar in a recipe with molasses will slow down an otherwise rapid and damaging release of sugar into the blood.

- Contains a balance of calcium and magnesium, which promotes calm mood and an ability to cope with stress, both important antiaging factors.
- Potassium content for good heart function and to prevent bloating and puffiness.
- A good vegetarian source of iron, essential for rejuvenating energy and the oxygenation of all skin cells and organs.

Practical tips:
Choose unsulfured molasses, made from the more mature sugar cane. It does not require the addition of the preservative sulfur dioxide, which can cause stomach upsets and headaches. Use as a sugar or syrup substitute.

Gingerbread

SERVES 9

7 tbsp unsalted butter, plus extra
   for greasing

heaping ¼ cup dark brown sugar

5 tbsp molasses

1 egg white

1 tsp almond extract

1¼ cups all-purpose flour, plus
   extra for dusting

¼ tsp baking soda

¼ tsp baking powder

pinch of salt

½ tsp allspice

½ tsp ground ginger

heaping 1 cup finely chopped
   apple, cooked

Method

1 Preheat the oven to 350°F/180°C. Grease a 9-inch/23-cm square, deep cake pan and line it with parchment paper. Put the butter, sugar, molasses, egg white, and almond extract into a food processor and blend until smooth.

2 In a separate bowl, sift the flour, baking soda, baking powder, salt, allspice, and ginger together. Add to the creamed mixture and beat together thoroughly. Stir in the chopped apples. Pour the mixture into the prepared cake pan.

3 Transfer to the preheated oven and bake for 10 minutes, or until golden brown. Remove from the oven and cut into 9 pieces. Transfer the squares to a wire rack and let them cool completely before serving.

88 HONEY

Raw honey is one of nature's oldest known antibacterial products. It destroys harmful invaders, keeping you young both inside and out.

Honey is created when the saliva of bees meets the pollen they collect from flowers, so the properties of a particular honey will reflect those of the flowers the bees have visited. In its raw state, it contains an array of antioxidants, such as chrysin and vitamin C, to help you stay young, but these properties are destroyed when it is excessively heated or processed. Manuka honey from New Zealand is the only honey that has been tested for its ability to destroy harmful bacteria, and batches of this are given a Unique Manuka Factor (UMF) according to strength. Manuka has been shown to be twice as effective as other honeys against *E. coli* and *Staphylococcus* bacteria, which commonly infect wounds.

- Raw honey contains propolis, which helps reduce inflammation and premature aging.
- Good-quality honey contains probiotic benefical bacteria lactobacilli and bifidobacteria to support youth-protecting immunity.
- When applied to the skin, it helps heal spots, burns, cuts, and sores that can age your appearance.

Practical tips:
Choose good-quality honey: look out for local raw and unprocessed varieties from farm stores. Darker kinds, such as buckwheat and sage, contain the most antioxidants, and the honey produced by flower-fed bees in the summer contains more beneficial bacteria. Use in place of sugar but sparingly, or you will set off sugar cravings.

DID YOU KNOW?

When mixed with water, honey creates antiseptic hydrogen peroxide, which can be applied directly to wounds to dry them out and keep them free from infection while they heal.

MAJOR NUTRIENTS PER 1 TBSP HONEY

Calories	45.5
Total fat	0 g
Protein	0.04 g
Carbohydrate	12.36 g
Fiber	0.03 g

Homemade granola

SERVES 6–8

3 cups rolled oats

2 Granny Smith or similar tart
   apples, peeled and diced

½ cup chopped dried figs

½ cup slivered almonds

2 tbsp good-quality honey

¼ cup cold water

1 tsp ground cinnamon

1 tsp vanilla extract

1 tsp butter, melted, for greasing

live Greek-style yogurt, for serving

Method

1 Preheat the oven to 325°F/160°C. Mix the oats, apples, figs, and
   almonds together in a large bowl. Bring the honey, water, cinnamon,
   and vanilla extract to a boil in a saucepan, then pour over the oat
   mixture, stirring well to make sure that all the ingredients are coated.

2 Lightly grease a large baking sheet with the butter and spread the
   oat mixture out evenly on the sheet. Bake for 40–45 minutes, or
   until the granola is golden brown, stirring with a fork from time to
   time to break up any lumps. Pour onto a clean baking sheet and
   let cool before storing in an airtight container. Serve sprinkled over
   bowls of fresh live Greek-style yogurt.

6

NUTS, SEEDS, AND OILS

Understanding that fat is a quality not a quantity issue is a major step in keeping young through nutrition. The organs and cells in your body are made of fats and need constant replenishment. Nuts, seeds, and oils are packed with healthy fats and a wide range of antiaging nutrients.

(S) Skin, hair, and nails

(M) Mobility and strength

(D) Digestive/detoxification health

(B) Brain health

(H) Heart health

(I) Immunity-supporting antioxidant

89 ALMONDS

Almonds are the perfect antiaging food. They are full of the protein, fiber, and omega-6 fatty acids that keep the body as young as possible for as long as possible.

MAJOR NUTRIENTS PER 3½ TBSP ALMONDS

Calories	174
Total fat	15 g
Monounsaturated fat	9.27 g
Omega-6 fatty acids	3,619 mg
Omega-9 fatty acids	9,182 mg
Protein	6.6 g
Carbohydrate	6 g
Fiber	3 g
Vitamin B_2	0.03 mg
Vitamin B_3	1.01 mg
Vitamin B_5	0.14 mg
Vitamin E	7.4 mg
Calcium	80 mg
Magnesium	80 mg
Potassium	211.5 mg
Phosphorus	145.2mg
Zinc	1.51 mg
Phytosterols	42.9 mg

All nuts are packed with healthy fats. Although the advice in this area can be confusing, the fact is that they encourage weight loss because they regulate blood-sugar levels and metabolism by providing a sustained fuel source. Extensive studies have also shown that eating almonds regularly lowers the body's levels of "bad" LDL cholesterol, as well as the risk of heart disease, gallstones, and diabetes. The omega-6 fatty acids play a part in heart health, too, and help to regulate mood, including the swings associated with premenstrual syndrome (PMS) and menopause. Almonds contain high levels of monounsaturated and oleic fatty acids, the substances found in olive oil, walnuts, and avocados, foods that are representative of the youth-preserving Mediterranean diet.

- High in phytosterols that prevent the absorption of cholesterol and support immunity to help you stay youthful.
- Contain an optimum, 1:1 ratio of calcium to magnesium for muscle and brain reactions.
- Vitamin E lubricates the skin, keeping it firm and protected from age spots.

Practical tips:
Almonds make a nutritious snack that wards off unhealthy sugar cravings. Eat them raw and avoid the less healthy, roasted or salted versions. Almonds may be soaked in water, which makes them easier to digest and for your body to access their nutrients.

Bean sprout, apricot, and almond salad

SERVES 4

¾ cup bean sprouts, washed
　　and dried
small bunch each of seedless black
　　and green grapes, halved
12 dried apricots, halved
¼ cup blanched
　　almonds, halved
pepper

Dressing
1 tbsp walnut oil
1 tsp sesame oil
2 tsp balsamic vinegar

Method
1　Place the bean sprouts in the bottom of a large salad bowl and sprinkle the grapes and apricots on top.
2　Place the oils and vinegar in a screw-top jar and shake vigorously to mix. Pour over the salad.
3　Scatter over the blanched almonds and season with pepper.

90

CHESTNUTS

Chestnuts are the only nuts that contain vitamin C. This combines with high levels of potassium to help protect the heart as it copes with the demands of growing older.

Chestnuts are energy-packed foods that release their starchy carbohydrates very slowly into the bloodstream, helping to regulate appetite and weight by keeping the lid on cravings for fattening and aging sugary foods. They offer a good alternative to grains, which may cause intolerances, or beans that can be difficult to digest. Chestnuts contain no cholesterol and their low fat content is mainly unsaturated, which adds to their beneficial heart-health profile. They also contain a good spread of the amino acids that make up the proteins we need to make hormones, bones, skin, and the neurotransmitters (brain chemicals) that keep you thinking youthfully and positively.

- The B vitamins enable you to produce the energy necessary to make constant repairs and fight aging throughout the body.
- Contains copper, which helps knit together the collagen that plumps up skin and prevents wrinkles.
- Manganese and vitamin B_3 content moves sugars into cells where they are needed for energy.

Practical tips:
Chestnuts can be bought whole and roasted for a tasty winter treat. Alternatively, you can buy them already peeled and vacuum-packed, which keep for a long time, and add to salads or stews as you like. Chestnuts are especially useful in vegetarian foods as they add flavor and create a denser texture.

DID YOU KNOW?

In order to feed their armies, the Romans and Alexander the Great planted chestnut trees across their campaign trails throughout Europe.

MAJOR NUTRIENTS PER ⅓ CUP CHESTNUTS

Calories	59
Total fat	0.375 g
Omega-6 fatty acids	132 mg
Omega-9 fatty acids	124 mg
Protein	0.26 g
Carbohydrate	13.2 g
Fiber	0 g
Vitamin C	12 mg
Vitamin B_3	0.33 mg
Vitamin B_5	0.14 mg
Vitamin B_6	0.1 mg
Potassium	145 mg
Copper	0.12 mg
Manganese	0.09 mg

Chestnut soup

SERVES 6

2 tbsp butter or 1 tbsp olive oil

1 onion, finely chopped

1 celery stalk, chopped

*7 oz/200 g vacuum-packed whole
    chestnuts*

*4 cups chicken or low-salt
    vegetable stock*

½ cup plain live yogurt

2 tbsp sherry (optional)

salt and pepper

*chopped fresh parsley,
    for garnishing*

Method

1 Melt the butter in a large saucepan over medium heat. Add the
   onion and celery and cook for 4–5 minutes, until softened.

2 Add the chestnuts and sauté for an additional 5 minutes. Pour
   in the stock and mix well. Bring to a boil and simmer for 20–25
   minutes, until the chestnuts are tender.

3 Transfer to a food processor or blender and process until smooth.
   Return to the rinsed-out saucepan. Add the yogurt to the soup,
   reheat, and season with salt and pepper to taste. Add the sherry,
   if using, and serve in warmed bowls garnished with the parsley.

91

WALNUTS

With their brain-boosting omega-3 fatty acids, quality protein, B vitamins, and zinc, walnuts make a potent mood food for youthful memory, focus, and concentration.

The nutrients in walnuts come together to make the sleep and mood neurotransmitter serotonin. Low levels of serotonin are associated with depression, insomnia, sugar cravings, bingeing, and overeating—all of which can lead to premature aging. The high levels of omega-3 fatty acids in walnuts also protect your arteries from the fat you get from less healthy foods. Research shows that adding just four of these wonder nuts a day to your diet can make a significant contribution to your blood profile, keeping your heart young and vital. Walnuts also contain the hormone melatonin, which regulates sleep patterns and helps you fall asleep, allowing you the opportunity for restoration and detoxification.

- A good source of the antioxidant compound ellagic acid, which stops cancer cells from replicating.
- Contains high levels of zinc, selenium, and phytosterols, which support a youthful immune system.
- High levels of omega-9 fatty acids (oleic acid) reduce the risk of arteriosclerosis, heart disease, and stroke.

Practical tips:
The high level of omega fatty acids in walnuts makes them quickly perishable. Store in airtight containers away from heat and light. They will keep for a longer time in the refrigerator, or you can even freeze them. To enjoy them at their freshest, buy whole and crack yourself whenever possible.

DID YOU KNOW?

Walnut shells are used in facial cleansers, as paint thickeners, to clean metals, and as filler for explosives. The inner husk is used to make a strong brown dye.

MAJOR NUTRIENTS PER ¼ CUP WALNUTS

Calories	196
Total fat	19.5 g
Monounsaturated fat	2.68 g
Omega-3 fatty acids	2,728 mg
Omega-6 fatty acids	11,428 mg
Omega-9 fatty acids	2,639 mg
Protein	4.57 g
Carbohydrate	4.1 g
Fiber	2 g
Vitamin B$_3$	0.34 mg
Vitamin B$_5$	0.17 mg
Vitamin B$_6$	0.16 mg
Magnesium	47.4 mg
Potassium	132 mg
Manganese	1.02 mg
Selenium	1.47 mcg
Zinc	0.93 mg
Phytosterols	32.4mg

Banana walnut bread

MAKES 1 LOAF

heaping 1 cup walnut oil

½ cup raw brown sugar

2 eggs

3 very ripe bananas, mashed

2 cups all-purpose flour

1 tsp baking soda

1 tsp baking powder

½ tsp salt

3 tbsp milk

2 tbsp plain live yogurt

½ tsp vanilla extract

½ cup walnuts, crushed

Method

1 Preheat the oven to 350°F/180°C. Grease a 9 x 5 x 3-inch/23 x 13 x 8-cm loaf pan. Using an electric mixer, beat the oil and sugar. Beat in the eggs and mashed bananas.

2 Combine the dry ingredients, then add to the banana mixture. Add the milk, yogurt, and vanilla and beat until blended. Stir in the crushed walnuts and pour the batter into the greased pan.

3 Bake for 50 minutes–1 hour, or until a skewer inserted into the middle comes out clean.

92 PECANS

Pecans contain the highest amount of antioxidant nutrients of any nut, making them highly protective against aging and disease.

MAJOR NUTRIENTS PER ⅓ CUP PECANS

Calories	207
Total fat	21.6 g
Monounsaturated fat	12.2 g
Omega-3 fatty acids	295 mg
Omega-6 fatty acids	6,189 mg
Omega-9 fatty acids	12,178 mg
Protein	2.7 g
Carbohydrate	4.15 g
Fiber	2.8 g
Vitamin B$_1$	0.19 mg
Vitamin B$_3$	0.35 mg
Vitamin B$_5$	0.25 mg
Folate	55 mcg
Magnesium	36 mg
Potassium	123 mg
Iron	1.4 mg
Manganese	1.35 mg
Zinc	1.35 mg
Phytosterols	32 mg

Pecans don't get the attention they deserve; studies have shown that a handful a day can help prevent heart disease and lower cholesterol. The amount of calories in pecans, and nuts in general, often leads to assumptions about weight gain, but it's important to remember that this high energy comes from the abundance of healthy fatty acids they contain. These fatty acids actually help raise metabolism and stop us craving the sugary foods that pile on the pounds and contribute to aging conditions, such as diabetes, arthritis, and heart disease. People who eat more than two portions of nuts a week are less prone to put on weight than those who avoid these nutrient-rich foods.

• High levels of omega-9 fatty acids (oleic acid) keep your skin clear and smooth.
• Good levels of balanced and high-quality protein ensure the necessary repairs are made to the body to hold back aging.
• Phytosterols work with high levels of antioxidants to discourage sensitivities and intolerances.

Practical tips:

Pecans are associated with sweet desserts, but they can be eaten on their own, or used as an interesting salad ingredient. Their rich, buttery taste gives them a luxurious quality that feels like a treat and they are a healthy alternative to candies or confectionery.

Nutty beet salad

SERVES 4

3 tbsp red wine vinegar or apple
  cider vinegar
3 cooked beet, grated
2 tart apples, such as Granny
  Smith
2 tbsp lemon juice
4 large handfuls mixed salad
  greens, for serving
4 tbsp pecans, for garnishing

Dressing

heaping ⅓ cup plain live yogurt
1 garlic clove, chopped
1 tbsp chopped fresh dill
salt and pepper

Method

1 Drizzle vinegar over the beet, cover with plastic wrap, and chill
  for at least 4 hours.
2 Core and slice the apples, place the slices in a dish, and drizzle
  with the lemon juice to prevent discoloration.
3 Combine the dressing ingredients in a small bowl. Remove
  the beet from the refrigerator and dress. Add the apples
  to the beet and mix gently to coat with the salad dressing.
4 To serve, arrange a handful of salad greens on each plate and
  top with a large spoonful of the apple-and-beet mixture.
5 Toast the pecans in a dry skillet over medium heat for 2 minutes,
  or until they begin to brown. Sprinkle over the beet and apple
  to garnish.

93 COCONUT

Coconut is an extremely dense energy source. It boosts the metabolism and satisfies hunger, helping to maintain youthful weight levels, energy, and vitality.

DID YOU KNOW?

Coconut is a native plant of the tropical Pacific, but also features in Indian writings as far back as 2,000 years ago, causing much debate as to its true origins.

MAJOR NUTRIENTS PER 1 CUP DRIED COCONUT, UNSWEETENED

Calories	660
Total fat	64.53 g
Lauric acid	28,629 mg
Caprylic acid	4,520 mg
Protein	6.88 g
Carbohydrate	23.65 g
Fiber	16.3 g
Vitamin B$_5$	0.8 mg
Magnesium	90 mg
Potassium	543 mg
Iron	3.32 mg
Manganese	2.75 mg
Selenium	18.5 mcg
Zinc	2.01 mg
Phytosterols	91 mg

Like nuts, coconut often gets a bad press, as it is high in fat. However, this is plant fat rather than animal fat, and as such it is easy for us to burn off as energy and digest. Cultures that include coconut regularly in their diets consistently show lower incidences of obesity, high cholesterol, heart disease, and diabetes. As this suggests, the antiaging benefits of this food are vast. It has been shown to prevent tumors, regulate cholesterol, normalize blood-sugar levels, and combat the aging effects of stress by nourishing tired adrenal glands. Coconut water has the same mineral levels as our blood so it assists rehydration, keeping skin smooth and plumped up, and reduces water retention.

- Good levels of phytosterols, zinc, and selenium help you combat aging elements in the environment.
- Contains lauric acid, also found in human breast milk, which protects against viruses and bacterial infections.
- Caprylic acid kills off fungal infections that can upset digestion and lower immune protection.

Practical tips:

The flesh that comes from inside the coconut may be eaten in its dried form or as milk, when the flesh has been mashed, steeped, and cooked. Coconut milk is a useful dairy alternative in smoothies and in curries. Dried coconut is best enjoyed unsweetened and, as a snack, will satisfy a sweet craving.

Coconut chile sauce

MAKES ABOUT 1¾ CUPS

½ fresh coconut or 1⅓ cups
   unsweetened dried coconut

2 fresh green chiles, seeded or not,
   to taste, and chopped

1-inch/2.5-cm piece fresh ginger,
   peeled and finely chopped

4 tbsp chopped fresh cilantro

2 tbsp lemon juice, or to taste

2 shallots, very finely chopped

Method

1 If you are using a whole coconut, use a hammer and nail to punch a hole in the "eye" of the coconut, then pour out the water from the inside and set aside. Use the hammer to break the coconut in half, then peel half and chop the flesh.

2 Put the coconut and chiles in a food processor and process for about 30 seconds, until finely chopped. Add the ginger, cilantro, and lemon juice and process again.

3 If the mixture seems too dry, stir in about 1 tablespoon of coconut water or water. Stir in the shallots and serve immediately, or cover and chill until required. This will keep its fresh flavor in the refrigerator for up to 3 days.

94

FLAX

Golden flaxseeds are one of nature's true superfoods. Soaking them bulks up the therapeutic fibers and helps you access their age-defying nutrients.

MAJOR NUTRIENTS PER 1½ TBSP FLAXSEEDS, GOLDEN

Calories	160
Total fat	42.16 g
Omega-3 fatty acids	22,813 mg
Omega-6 fatty acids	5,911 mg
Omega-9 fatty acids	7,359 mg
Protein	18.29 g
Carbohydrate	28.88 g
Fiber	27.3 g
Vitamin B$_1$	1.64 mg
Vitamin B$_3$	3.08 mg
Vitamin B$_5$	0.99 mg
Vitamin B$_6$	0.47 mg
Choline	78.7 mg
Calcium	255 mg
Magnesium	392 mg
Potassium	813 mg
Iron	5.73 mg
Selenium	25.4 mcg
Zinc	4.34 mg
Lutein/Zeaxanthin	651 mcg
Phytosterols	338 mg

Flaxseed (also known as linseed) that has been soaked to open up the tough outer covering and puff out the fiber inside is an age-old way of keeping the bowels regular. It combats constipation and diarrhea and ensures the rapid removal of aging toxins before they can cause the body any damage. The seed also binds to excess cholesterol in the body, which is then removed in support of heart and brain health. Regular consumption exercises the bowel muscle, improving digestive function long-term. The soaking process also produces a mucilage that coats the digestive tract wall, offering protection and healing, helping reduce food intolerances, and supporting the immune system to prevent premature aging.

- High levels of omega-3 fatty acids prevent aging inflammation and keep the skin supple and smooth.
- Contains lignans, which are a type of phytoestrogen. Phytoestrogen regulates hormones to assist both male and female sexual health and potency.
- High in antioxidants due to the lignans, phytosterols, lutein, and selenium, which give this food an excellent antiaging profile.

Practical tips:
Flaxseeds are either brown or golden, but the golden variety is easier to absorb. Soak for 10 minutes in warm water, then add 2 teaspoons—including the water—to oatmeal, cereal, a smoothie, or yogurt in order to get their therapeutic benefits.

Apple and vegetable smoothie

SERVES 1–2

1 tsp golden flaxseeds,
   plus extra to serve
1 apple, peeled, cored, and
   chopped
1 large carrot, chopped
1 celery stalk, chopped
½ fennel bulb, chopped

Method

1 Soak the flaxseeds for 10 minutes in warm water. Process or blend the flaxseeds, apple, carrot, celery, and fennel together.

2 Pour into glasses and sprinkle with flaxseeds to serve.

95

PUMPKIN SEEDS

Rich in protein, minerals, and omega fatty acids, pumpkin seeds are full of youth-enhancing nutrients and eating them will help you renew and revitalize.

MAJOR NUTRIENTS PER 2 TBSP PUMPKIN SEEDS

Calories	84
Total fat	6.9 g
Monounsaturated fat	2.43 g
Omega-6 fatty acids	3,105 mg
Omega-9 fatty acids	2,121 mg
Protein	4.5 g
Carbohydrate	1.6 g
Fiber	0.9 g
Vitamin B$_1$	0.04 mg
Vitamin B$_3$	0.74 mg
Vitamin B$_5$	0.11 mg
Magnesium	88.8 mg
Potassium	121 mg
Phosphorus	185 mg
Iron	1.32 mg
Manganese	0.68 mg
Selenium	1.4 mcg
Zinc	1.17 mg
Phytosterols	38.75 mg

Pumpkin seeds contain high levels of protein, essential in the renewal of skin and bone, and also in making the hormones and brain chemicals that we rely on to stay feeling energetic and mentally vibrant. The protein in the equivalent weight of pumpkin seeds contains more tryptophan than a glass of milk. Tryptophan is the amino acid, or protein building block, from which we make the brain chemical serotonin, which helps keep us positive and youthful in outlook. What's more, studies have shown that pumpkin seeds are as effective as some anti-inflammatory medications at reducing inflammation. While these medications may have a side effect of harming the joints, pumpkin seeds contain fatty acids and minerals that actively promote mobility.

• Contain phosphorus, magnesium, and vitamin B$_3$, which help the body replace any damaged bone.
• High levels of phytosterols, zinc, and selenium protect the male prostate gland.
• Soluble fiber keeps us free from the toxins that age us so quickly.

Practical tips:
Add seeds to salads, soups, and vegetables as a garnish. Although they are delicious roasted, it is best to add them to a meal after cooking as this retains the benefits of the omega-3 and omega-6 fatty acids, which are unstable in heat and light.

Pumpkin loaf

SERVES 6

½ cup (1 stick) butter, softened,
plus extra for greasing

1 lb 9 oz/700 g pumpkin flesh

scant ¾ cup raw brown sugar

2 eggs, lightly beaten

1½ cups all-purpose flour

1½ tsp baking powder

½ tsp salt

1 tsp ground allspice

2 tbsp pumpkin seeds

Method

1 Preheat the oven to 400°F/200°C. Grease a 9 x 5 x 3-inch/23 x 13 x 8-cm loaf pan.

2 Pare and skin the pumpkin, then chop the flesh into large pieces and wrap in greased foil. Cook in the oven for 30–40 minutes, until tender. Reduce the oven temperature to 325°F/160°C. Let the pumpkin cool completely before mashing well to make a thick paste.

3 In a bowl, cream the butter and sugar together until light and fluffy. Add the beaten eggs, a little at a time. Stir in the pumpkin paste, then sift in the flour, baking powder, salt, and allspice.

4 Fold the pumpkin seeds gently through the mixture in a figure-eight movement. Spoon the mixture into the prepared loaf pan. Bake in the oven for about 1¼–1½ hours, or until a skewer inserted into the center of the loaf comes out clean.

5 Transfer the loaf to a wire rack to cool, then serve, sliced and buttered, if liked.

96

TAHINI

Tahini is a delicious way to eat large quantities of the highly beneficial and therapeutic sesame seed.

MAJOR NUTRIENTS PER 1 TBSP DARK TAHINI

Calories	85.5
Total fat	7.2 g
Monounsaturated fat	2.7 g
Omega-6 fatty acids	3,098 mg
Omega-9 fatty acids	2,865 mg
Protein	2.67 g
Carbohydrate	3.92 g
Fiber	0.52 g
Vitamin B₁	0.19 mg
Vitamin B₂	0.07 mg
Vitamin B₃	0.88 mg
Vitamin B₅	0.10 mg
Vitamin B₆	0.02 mg
Folate	14.7 mcg
Calcium	63 mg
Phosphorus	112.8 mg
Potassium	62.1 mg
Iron	0.37 mg
Zinc	0.69 mg
Phytosterols	60 mg

Sesame seeds contain two exclusive compounds: sesamin and sesamolin, types of lignans that offer potent heart protection by regulating cholesterol and high blood pressure. They also revitalize vitamin E in your body to increase antioxidant activity, particularly in the skin, where it helps heal scars and blemishes, and prevent age spots. Sesame seeds have the highest levels of phytosterols of any food, vital for immune function and lowering cholesterol. Sesame seeds also contain the fat-soluble nutrients beta-carotene and vitamin E, which are important antioxidants.

- High levels of vitamin B_3, phosphorus, and calcium keep bones strong and young.
- Sesamin helps prevent damage in the liver from the toxins it is exposed to, supporting the organ's elimination of harmful, aging waste.
- High levels of omega-6 fatty acids and zinc promote a healthy hormone balance in women, which encourages positive mood and good bone health.

Practical tips:

Tahini, or sesame seed paste, makes a versatile addition to the kitchen pantry. It may be mixed with olive oil to make a dressing, used as a spread or to make hummus, or added to falafel, as is traditional in the Middle East. The darker version is preferable as it doesn't have the nutritious outer hull removed, but it can be a little rich for some tastes.

Hummus

SERVES 6

8 oz/225 g cooked or canned
  chickpeas, drained
⅔ cup tahini, well stirred
⅔ cup cold-pressed extra virgin
  olive oil, plus extra to serve
⅔ cup water, plus extra if needed
2 garlic cloves, coarsely chopped
6 tbsp lemon juice
1 tbsp chopped fresh mint
salt and pepper
1 tsp paprika, to serve

Method

1 Put the chickpeas, tahini, olive oil, and water into the blender and process briefly. Add the garlic, lemon juice, and mint and process until smooth.

2 Check the consistency of the hummus and, if it is too thick, add 1 tablespoon water and process again. Continue adding water, 1 tablespoon at a time, until the right consistency is achieved. Hummus should have a thick, coating consistency. Season with salt and pepper.

3 Spoon the hummus into a serving dish. Make a shallow hollow in the top and drizzle with 2–3 tablespoons olive oil. Cover with plastic wrap and chill until required. To serve, dust lightly with paprika.

97

DARK CHOCOLATE

Our love affair with chocolate is rooted in its health-giving properties. The cacao bean is loaded with nutrients, happy-mood chemicals, and youth-preserving antioxidants.

MAJOR NUTRIENTS PER 3½ oz/100 G DARK CHOCOLATE 70–85% COCOA SOLIDS

Calories	598
Total fat	42.63 g
Omega-9 fatty acids	12,652 mg
Protein	7.79 g
Carbohydrate	45.9 g
Fiber	10.9 g
Vitamin B_3	1.05 mg
Vitamin B_5	0.42 mg
Magnesium	228 mg
Potassium	716 mg
Phosphorus	308 mg
Iron	11.9 mg
Manganese	1.95 mg
Selenium	6.8 mcg
Zinc	3.31 mg
Caffeine	75.6 mg
Theobromine	448.8 mg

The bean from which we make our favorite confectionery is highly nutritious, being full of rejuvenating potassium, magnesium, vitamins B_3 and B_5, zinc, and selenium. However, its true potency comes from its high antioxidant content. Chocolate contains more than four times the catechins present in green tea and twice as much as in red wine. These substances lower the risk of both heart attacks and cancer by reducing inflammation and helping renew blood vessels, skin, and bone. More immediately, eating dark chocolate releases our beta-endorphins, or "happy chemicals."

- Caffeine and theobromine can boost energy and, in moderation, help balance blood sugar and so promote weight loss.
- Chocolate can improve quality of life, which is vital for staying young. Many people find it as pleasurable as sex.
- Contains healthy monounsaturated fats, shown to keep the heart youthful and strong.

Practical tips:
The health benefits only apply to good-quality dark chocolate: milk and sugar negate these. Eating dark chocolate with at least 70 percent cocoa solids—with nuts for extra benefits—will raise your antioxidant levels, but chocolate also has a high caffeine content, so avoid it late at night if you have sleep problems. An average small bar of chocolate contains the equivalent amount of caffeine of a third of a cup of coffee.

Mole sauce

SERVES 6–10

9 mixed chiles, soaked in hot water
   for 30 minutes and drained
1 onion, sliced
2–3 garlic cloves, crushed
heaping ¾ cup sesame seeds
heaping ⅓ cup toasted slivered
   almonds
1 tsp ground coriander
4 cloves
½ tsp pepper
2–3 tbsp olive oil
1¼ cups low-salt chicken
   or vegetable stock
1 lb/450 g ripe tomatoes, peeled
   and chopped
2 tsp ground cinnamon
⅓ cup raisins
1 cup pumpkin seeds
2 oz/55 g 70% minimum cocoa
   solids dark chocolate, broken
   into pieces
1 tbsp red wine vinegar

Method

1 Put the chiles into a blender with the onion, garlic, sesame seeds, almonds, coriander, cloves, and pepper and process to form a thick paste. Heat the oil in a saucepan, add the paste, and cook for 5 minutes. Add the stock with the tomatoes, cinnamon, raisins, and pumpkin seeds. Bring to a boil, reduce the heat, and simmer, stirring occasionally, for 15 minutes.

2 Add the chocolate and vinegar to the sauce. Cook gently for 5 minutes, then use as required. It is usually served with poultry.

98

COCONUT OIL

Cooking with coconut oil is a sure way to reduce your exposure to the aging free radicals that are produced when roasting, pan-frying, and baking.

Whenever we cook with oil, the heat causes some damage to the oil's fat molecules, which has a knock-on effect in our bodies. The free radicals produced can damage our body tissues and make us more susceptible to cancer, heart disease, and osteoporosis. Of all the saturated fats, coconut oil is the least prone to damage by heat, light, and oxygen, and can be heated to temperatures as high as 375°F/190°C. Because it is so stable, it keeps for a very long time. Coconut oil contains about 60 percent medium-chain triglycerides (MCTs), plant-based fats, which raise metabolism and cannot be stored as fat in our bodies. Researchers have found that in countries where breast milk is high in MCTs, the population as a whole demonstrates a better quality of aging.

- The fats in coconut oil help feed the lining of the digestive tract, ensuring good digestion and the elimination of aging toxins.
- Has been shown to assist thyroid function and regulate metabolism and mood, keeping us both trim and happy.

Practical tips:
Coconut oil, which becomes a clear liquid when heated, can be used in all kinds of cooking and doesn't retain any of the coconut flavor from the flesh. It does behave differently from other oils, however, so a little experimentation may be necessary. Choose an unprocessed variety, and avoid any that have been hydrogenated or contain preservatives.

DID YOU KNOW?

Many Pacific Island countries use coconut oil as fuel for cars, trucks, buses, and generators, and also as engine lubricant.

MAJOR NUTRIENTS PER 1 TBSP COCONUT OIL

Calories	129
Total fat	15 g
Lauric acid	6.69 g
Caprylic acid	1.125 g
Myristic acid	2.5 g
Omega-6 fatty acids	270 mg
Omega-9 fatty acids	870 mg
Protein	0 g
Carbohydrate	0 g
Fiber	0 g

Thai green chicken curry

SERVES 4

2 tbsp coconut oil

2 tbsp Thai green curry paste

1 lb 2 oz/500 g skinless, boneless
 chicken breasts, cut into cubes

2 kaffir lime leaves, roughly torn

1 lemongrass stalk, finely chopped

1 cup coconut milk

16 baby eggplants, halved

2 tbsp Thai fish sauce

fresh Thai basil sprigs and thinly
 sliced kaffir lime leaves,
 for garnishing

Method

1 Heat the oil in a preheated wok or large heavy-bottom skillet.
Add the Thai curry paste and stir-fry briefly until all the aromas
are released.

2 Add the chicken, lime leaves, and lemongrass and stir-fry for
3–4 minutes, until the meat is beginning to color. Add the
coconut milk and eggplants and simmer gently for 8–10 minutes,
or until tender.

3 Stir in the fish sauce and serve immediately, garnished with Thai
basil sprigs and lime leaves.

99

FLAXSEED OIL

Flaxseed oil is one of the best plant sources of anti-inflammatory omega-3 fatty acids. These balance with the omega-6 oil content to create a superior antiaging ingredient.

MAJOR NUTRIENTS PER 1 TBSP FLAXSEED OIL

Calories	132
Total fat	0.43 g
Monounsaturated fat	4.63 g
Omega-3 fatty acids	7,995 mg
Omega-6 fatty acids	1,905 mg
Omega-9 fatty acids	3,029 mg
Protein	1.19 g
Carbohydrate	11.58g
Fiber	0.5 g
Vitamin C	0.05 mg
Vitamin B₁	0.05 mg
Vitamin B₂	0.04 mg
Vitamin B₃	0.64 mg
Vitamin B₅	0.21 mg
Vitamin B₆	0.06 mg
Folate	27.6mcg
Calcium	9.9 mg
Magnesium	24 mg
Potassium	69 mg
Iron	0.74 mg
Manganese	0.9 mg
Selenium	2.7 mcg
Zinc	0.75 mg
Lutein/Zeaxanthin	31.5 mcg

Most modern diets are much higher in omega-6 fatty acids than omega 3 and this can cause health problems and the dry skin and poor concentration associated with omega-3 fatty acid deficiency. The omega oil ratio in flaxseed oil provides the optimum support for heart, joint, and brain function. Flaxseed oil is also rich in lignans, renowned for their antioxidant, antiviral, antibacterial, and anticancer actions. Lignans help regulate sex hormones and combat premenstrual syndrome, menopausal symptoms, prostate problems, and hormone-sensitive cancers like breast and prostate. Flaxseeds contain by far the highest amount of these valuable substances—ten times more than any other seed, grain, or vegetable.

- Important rejuvenating food for people who do not get their essential omega-3 fatty acids from oily fish.
- Excellent digestive tract-healing action that stops harmful elements from entering the bloodstream.
- High in heart-revitalizing oleic acid (omega-9 fatty acid), the same found in olive oil.

Practical tips:
Flaxseed oil is easily damaged by heat, light, or oxygen. To preserve its benefits, it needs to be stored in dark glass bottles and cannot be used for any type of cooking. It makes a healthy base for salad dressings, and can also be added to juices or smoothies, which slows the release of their sugars into the bloodstream.

Watercress and carrot juice

SERVES 4

heaping 2 cups unsweetened
  carrot juice
10 sprigs watercress, plus extra
  sprigs for garnishing
1 tbsp lemon juice
1 tsp cold-pressed flaxseed oil

Method

1 Pour the carrot juice into a food processor. Add the watercress, lemon juice, and flaxseed oil and process until smooth. Transfer to a pitcher, cover with plastic wrap, and chill in the refrigerator for at least 1 hour, or until required.

2 When the mixture is thoroughly chilled, pour into glasses and garnish with sprigs of fresh watercress. Serve at once.

100 OLIVE OIL

Olive oil is the foundation of the healthy Mediterranean diet. It is well documented for its contribution to the longevity of the population.

The monounsaturated fats, flavones, quercetin, and omega-9 fatty acids (oleic acid) in olive oil create a heady combination of protective nutrients, particularly famed for their heart health properties. A specific compound in olive oil called hydroxytyrosol protects fats in the arteries from being damaged, which halts the progression of heart disease. Quercetin is one of many polyphenols in olive oil that stimulates the enzymes shown to extend the lifespan of cells by helping them repair damage. This work is crucial to your body's ability to continually renew and hold back aging. Olive oil also contains a newly discovered compound called oleocanthal that has the same anti-inflammatory action as ibuprofen.

- Allows the absorption of fat-soluble nutrients, such as vitamins A, and E and carotenoids, which encourages glowing skin.
- Vitamin E and omega-6 fatty acids keep the complexion youthful by helping the skin stay soft, smooth, and blemish-free.

Practical tips:
There are so many ways to include olive oil in your diet: in cooking, salads, dressings, and dips. For the best health benefits and taste, choose organic, cold-pressed, extra virgin oils. As with most foods, you get what you pay for. Olive oil stays stable up to about 325°F/160°C, so is suitable for use in cooking up to a moderate heat.

DID YOU KNOW?

Of the 750 million olive trees in the world, 95 percent grow in the Mediterranean. As much as 60 percent of the land in Greece is given over to this crop.

MAJOR NUTRIENTS PER 1 TBSP OLIVE OIL

Calories	132
Total fat	15 g
Monounsaturated fat	4.62 g
Omega-6 fatty acids	1,464 mg
Omega-9 fatty acids	10,689 mg
Protein	0 g
Carbohydrate	0 g
Fiber	0 g
Vitamin E	2.15 mg

Olive oil crushed sweet potatoes

SERVES 4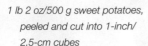

1 lb 2 oz/500 g sweet potatoes,
    peeled and cut into 1-inch/
    2.5-cm cubes
heaping ¾ cup low-salt vegetable
    stock
3 tbsp cold-pressed extra virgin
    olive oil
1 shallot, finely chopped
2 garlic cloves, finely chopped
1 tsp dried or 2 tsp fresh thyme
    leaves
1 tsp sweet paprika
1 tsp crushed coriander seeds
pepper

Method

1 Place the sweet potatoes in a saucepan with just enough stock
to cover. Bring to a simmer and cook for 7 minutes, or until nearly
tender (do not overcook).

2 Heat 1 tablespoon of the oil in a skillet and stir-fry the shallot
over medium heat for 3 minutes to soften. Add the garlic, thyme,
paprika, and coriander seeds to the skillet. Stir for 1 minute.

3 Add the sweet potatoes to the skillet and stir gently for
2–3 minutes, until the potatoes start to break up. Pour over the
remaining olive oil, a little salt (only if needed), and plenty of black
pepper. Stir for an additional 1 minute and then very lightly crush
with a potato masher if necessary to break up the potatoes further.
Transfer to a serving dish and serve.

GLOSSARY

Allergies Immune system reactions that set off aging inflammation and can be triggered by foods or environmental factors.

Amino acids The 22 "building blocks" of protein that keep bone, skin, and muscles repaired. Eight are essential and we can only derive them from food.

Antioxidant Substances that stop the damaging effects of free radicals, such as toxins and pollutants.

"Bad" LDL cholesterol Low-density lipoproteins (LDL) transport cholesterol from the liver to the heart. If higher than "good" HDL cholesterol, the risk of heart disease increases.

Beta-carotene See carotenoids—an orange pigment.

Bioflavonoid/flavonoid Types of polyphenols that have positive effects on the immune system response to allergies, inflammation, and microbes.

Carbohydrate The basis of all plant foods (vegetables, fruit, grains, beans, nuts, and seeds), which break down into the simple sugars we use for fuel.

Carotenoids Chemical oily pigments that give fruit and vegetables their yellow/red/orange colors. They are antioxidants that protect fats in the body.

Catechin A type of bioflavonoid, shown to have specific antiaging benefits for the heart, skin, and immune system.

Cholesterol An essential fatty substance, consumed in foods of animal origin, that we use to make certain hormones, vitamin D, and new cells. Too much cholesterol is associated with heart disease.

Circulation The system by which blood is pumped by the heart around the body, delivering oxygen and nutrients to all cells.

Collagen The protein substance from which all new cells and tissues are made.

Detoxification The process in the liver and all individual cells by which harmful and aging toxins are broken down and eliminated.

Digestion The process by which we breakdown, absorb, and assimilate the food we eat to derive the nutrients that we need.

Ellagic acid A polyphenol antioxidant that supports antiaging by strengthening immunity and improving detoxification capacity.

Essential fatty acid/essential fat/EFA Essential polyunsaturated fats that the body needs for smooth skin and immunity.

Estrogen A sexual hormone produced by women in the ovaries. Levels need to be balanced to reduce the risk of hormone-sensitive cancers. Declining levels after the menopause are linked with osteoporosis and depression.

Fats Substances that provide a waterproof structure to cells and skin, keeping them supple and young. They also provide energy for the brain and heart and need to be eaten in the correct amounts for good health and youth.

Free radicals Unstable molecules from pollution, toxins, sunlight, stress, and electrical activity that, if not quenched by antioxidants from food, can hasten the aging process by damaging cells.

Glucosinolates Sulfur-based compounds found in brassicas, such as cabbage, which support detoxification and the immune system function.

Glycemic index/GI A comparative measure of the speed at which plant foods break down their carbohydrates into sugars and release into the bloodstream; lower, slower values are best for antiaging.

"Good" HDL cholesterol High-density lipoproteins (HDL) carry cholesterol from the heart to the liver. Higher levels of HDL rather than LDL cholesterol may help protect against heart disease.

Homocysteine A naturally occurring substance that can build up in the blood; raised levels are associated with heart disease, bone loss, and dementia.

Immune system The body system responsible for protection against aging invaders, such as bacteria and viruses.

Indole-3-Carbinol/indoles Type of glucosinalate.

Inflammation The body's natural immune reaction to stress and illness that causes soreness, redness, and irritation.

Insoluble fiber Fiber, or "roughage," from the indigestible cellulose part of the plant foods that we eat. It does not get digested, but removes toxins and bulks stools to help digestion and detoxification.

Insulin The hormone produced by the pancreas that moves sugars from the bloodstream into cells to be used for energy.

Intolerances Immune system reactions that set off aging inflammation; slower than allergic reactions and can be moderated.

Inulin A type of "prebiotic" dietary fiber that feeds the "probiotic" beneficial digestive system bacteria, a crucial factor for longevity.

Isothiocyanates See glucosinolates.

Lignan The major phytoestrogen that helps balance sexual hormones in women and men.

L-tyrosine/tyrosine An amino acid needed for energy, brain function, and metabolism.

Lutein See carotenoids—a yellow pigment.

Lycopene See carotenoids—a red pigment.

Metabolism The rate at which we burn off the food we eat as fuel to make energy in all organs and cells.

Minerals Natural elemental substances found in the soil that enter the food chain; "essential" minerals, such as magnesium and zinc, must be got from food.

Monounsaturated fatty acids/ fats Fats that are solid when refrigerated but oily at room temperature and are associated with lower heart disease risk.

Oleic acid A type of monounsaturated fat, also known as omega-9 fatty acid, found in the highest quantities in olive oil.

Omega-3 fatty acids Polyunsaturated fats that help prevent and reduce inflammation and disease, necessary for strong immunity and heart function.

Omega-6 fatty acids Polyunsaturated fats that help prevent and reduce inflammation.

Omega-9 fatty acids See oleic acid.

ORAC The comparative measure of Oxygen Radical Absorbance Capacity, an international scale of the strength of antioxidant action in food.

Pectin A type of soluble fiber shown to reduce "bad" cholesterol levels and remove harmful, aging toxins from the body.

Phytoestrogen Plant variety of estrogen that helps balance sexual hormones.

Phytonutrient Chemical compounds known to have health and antiaging benefits, but which differ from vitamins and minerals.

Polyphenol A group of plant chemicals that includes bioflavonoids, polyphenols, and ellagic acid; vital for staying young through their actions on immunity and circulation.

Polyunsaturated fat Type of fats that act as oils and stay liquid even when refrigerated. Found in oils from plant foods, they are usually high in omega-6 fatty acids, with some omega-3 fatty acids.

Prebiotics Types of soluble fiber from plant foods that support beneficial bacteria in the intestines.

Proanthocyanidin A purple, red, or blue powerful antioxidant food pigment that also supports circulation.

Probiotics Beneficial, "friendly" digestive bacteria that support digestion, immunity, and detoxification, as well as helping to reduce allergies, intolerances and inflammation.

Protein The substance that we eat, mainly from animal foods but also from plants, to make body structures like skin, bone, teeth, muscle, and ligaments.

Quercetin An antioxidant bioflavonoid that reduces inflammation and allergic responses.

Rutin An antioxidant bioflavonoid related to quercetin that reduces risk factors for heart disease.

Saponins Antioxidants with natural antibiotic actions that remove cholesterol from the body and protect the digestive tract.

Saturated fats Fats that remain solid at room temperature and are mainly found in foods of animal origin; we need some for good health but in lower amounts than omega fatty acids/polyunsaturates.

Serotonin A neurotransmitter or brain chemical that regulates mood, sleep, appetite, and sexual desire.

Sinigrin Type of glucosinolate.

Soluble fiber A type of fiber that breaks down to support digestive health and acts as "prebiotic" fiber to feed our beneficial digestive system bacteria.

Sterols/plant sterols/ phytosterols Plant compounds that help reduce "bad" cholesterol levels and support immunity.

Sulforaphane Type of glucosinolate.

Toxic metals Naturally occurring harmful minerals, such as mercury, lead, and cadmium, that damage cells and cause aging.

Tryptophan An amino acid that helps to regulate appetite and reduce sugar cravings by producing the neurotransmitter serotonin.

Vitamins Chemicals that are crucial for body functions and, therefore, health and vitality; we cannot make them in our bodies but must eat them daily in food.

Zeaxanthin See carotenoids.

INDEX